END

I believe the message of this book is both timely and prophetic for the days we are living in. It is in the place of intimacy with the Lord where we are changed into His likeness. It is in the place of intimacy that His power and anointing begin to flow through us in the most wonderful ways. I encourage you to live out the message of this book and watch your life be radically transformed.

—*Carol Arnott*
Catch the Fire, Toronto, Ontario, Canada

Before we can release God's love to the world, we must first let God's love touch us. That is what being a "laid-down lover" is all about. James and Michal Ann Goll have been a rare breed of a husband-wife team, showing us how to dwell in the secret place of the most high God. Sweet Michal Ann now basks in unfeigned worship directly before the throne while James continues His pilgrimage on this side. But together they touched the lives of many and most importantly, touched the very heart of God Himself.

—*Heidi Baker*
Iris Ministries International, Pemba, Mozambique

I have personally had the honor of knowing James and the late Michal Ann Goll for more than forty years. They served with me in Kansas City for over a decade in various capacities, always demonstrating a lavish love for Jesus. I commend to you these vintage writings in this Women on the Frontlines series of books. The Golls are among those who long to see Jesus receive the rewards for His suffering. I give a hearty *amen* to Michal Ann's lineage and legacy of her ministry and the teachings found in these books.

—*Mike Bickle*
Founder of IHOP-KC, Kansas City, Missouri

Michal Ann Goll has written beautifully, calling us to the secret place. With many anecdotes and examples from both the past and the present from those who made it to the secret place, Michal Ann is calling us to follow in their footsteps. I believe she is articulating the call of the Holy Spirit—He wants all of us to enter into deeper intimacy with God.

—*Wesley and Stacey Campbell*
Be a Hero Ministries, Kelowna, British Columbia, Canada

This book about women of prayer, *A Call to the Secret Place,* brings you directly into God's presence as you come to know the women "saints" Michal Ann selected to write about. Some lived several hundred years ago; others are contemporary women who have responded to God's call to the secret place. As you read, follow your own desire to enter God's quiet sanctuary. You will yearn to open yourself more to His voice, His direction, His love. Abandon yourself to His call.

—*Quin Sherrer,*
Author of many books about prayer

Few people have touched my life like Michal Ann Goll. Her life, her love for God, her ministry, and her writings have left our lovely Savior's impact upon me. For years, James and Michal Ann have been friends of Life Center in Harrisburg, Pennsylvania, and of my husband, Charles, and I. Though Michal Ann has graduated to heaven, I continue to read these Women on the Frontlines series books over and over. You will want to also.

—*Anne Stock*
Life Center, Harrisburg, Pennsylvania

Michal Ann poured out her heart in a vulnerable, even tender way to her fellow sisters in Christ. It is almost as if she is God's cheerleader for the reader even to this day, exhorting them, "Go on, Sister, you can do it!" Let love take action in your life and make a difference for Jesus Christ's sake!

—*Cindy Jacobs*
Generals International, Red Oak, Texas

WOMEN ON THE FRONTLINES

A Call to the Secret Place

Pursuing the Prize of God's Presence

James & Michal Ann Goll

BroadStreet
PUBLISHING

BroadStreet Publishing Group, LLC
Racine, Wisconsin, USA
BroadStreetPublishing.com

A Call to the Secret Place
Pursuing the Prize of God's Presence

Cover design by Chris Garborg at www.garborgdesign.com
Interior by Katherine Lloyd at www.theDESKonline.com

Printed in the United States of America
16 17 18 19 20   5 4 3 2 1

DEDICATION

We dedicate this book of the Women on the Frontlines series to our mothers and grandmothers, who
all walked in the faith—our Willard and McCoy and
Goll and Burns heritage. These godly women blazed
a trail for us, and we have walked in the footsteps of
giants. Our desire is that we in turn can blaze a trail
for the generations that follow us.

CONTENTS

FOREWORD

━

Someone asked me, "Tell me about Michal Ann Goll. What was she like?" I closed my eyes and thought back. As the memories flooded in, the tears welled up and I couldn't speak.

Michal Ann Goll. The first time I laid eyes on her, she was preaching at a women's conference...while baking bread, no less! She was demonstrating the process of turning raw grain into finished bread; it was an allegory of the Christian walk. As she wiped her flour-covered hands on her backside, I thought to myself, *I'm gonna* love *this girl!*

And indeed I did. This spunky, sweet Missouri-born mother of four always had a smile on her face. I will always remember her walking around singing and worshipping. I never heard a negative word out of her mouth about anyone. Perhaps that was one reason why the secret place seemed always so near to her. Michal Ann didn't just talk about the secret place; she *lived* in it.

The first time I visited in the Goll home, they had just moved into a small house with their four children. It was crowded, but the fruit of the Spirit was everywhere. The first night I was in their home, God had a word that He would give them a lovely house on a hill with lots of green grass on its acreage, with horses on it. Michal Ann began to cry, because she said this had always been her dream.

As with most ministries, their finances were never on the high side. When Michal Ann was asked, "How will this happen?" her answer would be, "I'll discuss it with God." Well, she must have done that, because the house and acreage became a beautiful reality. As she would later say, "It was birthed in my secret place."

Michal Ann has called me a "grandmother of the prayer shield." And indeed I have written books on prayer and intercession. But I have never met a Christian yet who doesn't yearn for that call to the secret place. Some are too afraid to seek it. Some just don't want to take up the challenge. But some are like this deep, passionate, sensitive friend of mine—they don't just visit the secret place. They accept the call, walk the walk, and *live* there.

Six weeks before her death, I saw Michal Ann seated alone at a conference spending time communing with her God. She was very weak and ill, yet her arms and face were lifted up to the Lord in prayer and worship. It seemed such a holy place she was abiding in, enveloped by His presence. Her life truly embodied that high call. This was my friend, Michal Ann Goll...so down to earth, and yet so at home in heavenly places.

If you have a secret place, few, if any, will even know about it. When God calls us to a secret place with Him, it's not something we advertise. Instead, we go quietly into that place where we meet with Him face to face. This book will encourage, teach, and guide you to your own secret place, and it will bless all fellow pilgrims and friends of the secret place.

Thus is the life of my friend and her dear husband, James. Together they lived the message in this book. I miss Michal Ann. But her prayers live on. They live on today in her children, in the Women on the Frontlines movement she birthed, and in her writings. You hold in your hand a key to the best place you will ever know—*A Call to the Secret Place* just for you.

Elizabeth (Beth) Alves
Founder of Increase International
Author of Mighty Prayer Warrior

INTRODUCTION

James W. Goll
(written on behalf of Michal Ann Goll for this edition)

I found my secret place with God in nature. When I was growing up, I used to spend hours sitting in the woods with my dear mother, Dorris Grace McCoy Willard, watching and listening to the chirping birds together. Those were priceless days spent together just "being," with very little talk but a whole lot of observing, patiently waiting, just enjoying nature and God.

Later, I spent hours in our little barn that we rebuilt on our "Field of Dreams" in the beautiful rolling hills of Franklin, Tennessee. I learned many lessons there in solitude in that humble abode. I loved just "being" there with God, in the courts of His presence.

That is what God wants from each of us. Just "being with Him." He has been my closest friend since I was a child, and He will forever be my closest friend. What an honor it is to bring to you, along with the help my devoted husband, Jim (James to most of you), this Women on the Frontlines series of books. These chapters are like pages torn off from my own personal progression of life and ministry. I will take you on a journey from the transformational understandings in *A Call to Courage* to the fundamental essence of life in God found in *A Call to the Secret Place*. It all culminates in my ultimate love and call in life, *A Call to Compassion*.

Will you go on a journey with me? Will you follow in the footsteps of another pilgrim? Come along on an adventure of a lifetime in this series of books—written for men as well as women—Women on the Frontlines.

Part One

"Come Up Here"

✝

Chapter One

WHEN I'M CALLING YOU

The gospel is so simple and real. God loves us enormously; it's as though He has decided to leave us love notes everywhere. Whenever you open your heart to see and hear Him, He is there. It's wonderful to look back over your life and see those hidden messages strategically placed— especially when you did not notice them earlier.

I have one such love note I'd like to share with you. When I was growing up, my family enjoyed watching Jeanette MacDonald and Nelson Eddy movies. Jeanette MacDonald had a beautiful operatic voice and she seemed to be a Christian. When her lovely voice was blended with Nelson Eddy's rich baritone, the musical match was just heavenly.

One of their movies was *Rose-Marie,* known for the song, "Indian Love Call." Set in Canada, it is a romantic love story between a Canadian Royal Mounted police officer and a professional opera singer. At one point, the couple stands at a breathtaking scenic high point in the Canadian mountains, looking down into the valley. The Mountie teaches a bit of Indian folklore by singing "Indian Love Call," and the song captures the woman's heart. They fall deeply in love.

When a conflict threatens to separate the lovers forever, the opera singer (Jeanette MacDonald) returns to the same mountain peak. In hope that her voice will be able to find him, tearfully she sings "Indian Love Call" into the depths of the valley below. Her love is expressed in every line. As she sings, the sound of her voice echoes through the valley to the mountain on the other side. The hills echo back each note, each word… "When I'm calling you / Will you answer true? / That means I'm offering my love to you. / To be your own….When you hear my love call ringing clear, / And I hear your answering echo, so dear….You belong to me. / I belong to you!"

Merely typing those words brings such warmth and tenderness into my heart, because I now can see something in those words that I didn't see as a child. I hear a voice calling me; it is asking for a response to a song I've been taught by the greatest romantic of them all. If you listen, you'll hear it too. Can you hear Him singing your name over the mountaintops? He is aching to hear your heart's response to Him. "When I'm calling you…Will you answer true…?" He's calling!

If you learn to listen, and if you are still, you will hear the voice that calls each one of us. And if you follow, you will find the secret place where the One who is love eternal dwells.

There alone, in His everlasting arms, will you find strength and peace. There you will be shown the wonders of His love.

The question is: how do we find our way to the secret place where God abides?

Selah

In recent decades, we have been learning great lessons about prayer. Many ministries have sprung up to teach Christians how to be prayer warriors—how to pray for the lost, our schools, our towns and cities, and our nation. Yet, for all our praying, many of us lack a sense of closeness and intimacy with God to whom we pray. We may have no clue how to truly find God in our prayer time. With all our understanding about God's awesome power, it's as if we've lost sight of God Himself and His longing to be intimate with us.

If we want to find God in our everyday experience and sense His real presence throughout life's struggles and joys, we must learn about a kind of prayer few of us understand: the prayer of inner quiet.

In the psalms, we discover long lists of God's amazing attributes and His great and mighty acts. We read, "You are the God who does wonders," "You have demonstrated your power among the people," and "With Your mighty arm You have redeemed Your people, the sons of Jacob and Joseph." We get into the pace of those words, imagining a God who is always on the move. Unfortunately, often we miss the all-important instruction at the end: *selah*—"pause a minute and calmly think about what you've just read."

In this tender instruction, we hear the echo of God's

voice calling to us from out of time, calling us to come apart to be alone with Him. But we miss His voice in the midst of our busy days; we run until we drop and then we get up the next day and start all over again.

Although we often complain about our demanding, stressed-out lives, most of us have become accustomed to the frantic pace. We scarcely know what to do with ourselves when things slow down. Some of us are even afraid to slow down, afraid of what will happen. Our running keeps us just ahead of the wind at our backs. And if we should suddenly stop, the whirlwind of promises we've made and responsibilities we've picked up—everything that's swirling in our wake—will catch up with us. Up to now, we've kept just a step ahead, but in a moment it could suddenly overtake us.

At the same time, we sense our own desire to retreat to the wonderful spirit-place, the quiet sanctuary where God abides. Even if we sense His call, we object, "I don't have the time!" when someone encourages us to give prayer greater space in our lives. Giving up in frustration before we even start, we never answer God's love-call.

Learn to Take the Time

No matter how busy your lifestyle has been, you can learn how to enter the secret place with God. You can know His real presence with you every day.

Learning to change the lifestyle you've been living is going to take time. Be patient with yourself. At the same time, learn how to be patient in waiting upon God. Although God is always present with you, coming into the secret place with Him is one thing you cannot hurry. You're not going to get there if you're a speed-reader or if you're a great administrator who lives by a checklist. None of the things you have learned how to do to "make things happen" will help you come into this place in spirit.

You will only find your way to the secret place with God if you learn to take the time.

Nothing Is Impossible

Time is hard to find, it seems. I assure you, I know all about the issue of time...and the lack thereof.

Some years ago, my husband, James, came home on fire after being at a fantastic Christian conference. He could hardly sit down. He walked from room to room, reviewing all the amazing details. "God was so great!" he kept saying. "This amazing thing happened, and that miracle took place."

All the while I was thinking, *Please! Don't tell me another word.* You see, at the time we were between houses, living with our four kids in someone else's basement. I was homeschooling a first grader and getting up in the night with our youngest, in addition to keeping up with the two in between. Every ounce of energy and focus was going to the kids. I was so hungry to be with God, but I didn't have time to go off on a weekend retreat. James was so elated, and all I could do was listen and feel miserable.

When he finally left the room, I leaned my head against the wall and silently cried, my tears releasing to God the depth of my hunger. I felt desperate, because it seemed that I could do nothing to find a spare minute to be alone with Him.

Just then the Lord came to me in my desperation, and in that still small voice inside, He said, *Ann, I know all that. I am the God of the impossible, and what you think is impossible is possible with Me. I will come to you. I will visit you in the night.*

I wasn't even sure I understood what He meant. But the most amazing thing began to happen. Night after night I began to dream. One night I dreamed that a dear, sweet old gentleman came to me. I knew who He was at once. He was so kind and loving, and He loved the fragrance of my hair. He wanted me to simply lean near and hug Him, so He could smell it. I had never noticed that my hair had any kind of scent, but He did. He knew everything about me. In this way, night after night, God came wooing. We went on long walks down country lanes, and He told me how precious I am to Him and revealed how He cherishes me. I was given a gift of seeing myself through His loving eyes.

Of course I believe that perhaps these dreams were unusual. But I know that I am no more unique or specially favored by God than anyone else. He simply had a specific way of revealing His love to me at that time of my life, and I know He has a very special, personal way to reveal Himself to you too.

I'm telling you about my experience so that you will know one thing for sure: with God, nothing is impossible. Even though you may feel like your schedule is too full or too busy, and you don't know how you can squeeze out an additional moment, God Himself can make a way. In fact, He is already seeking out the times and places where He can

WHEN I'M CALLING YOU

meet alone with you. He's looking for the tiniest opening in your day or your night, when He can make His wonderful presence known to you.

Entering In

The dreams gave me a very real assurance of God's love and presence, although they did not last. They served as a catalyst, an invitation. They spurred me on in my pursuit of God, because they showed me that intimacy with Him was absolutely possible, regardless of where I was living, how sleep deprived I was, or what kind of daily stress I was experiencing. I wished I could have stayed in that wonderful secret place with Him forever, but it did not happen automatically. I had to learn how to take practical steps to meet with my God who so obviously longs to meet with me.

This is true for each one of us. How do we begin?

First, we must stop assuming that we need to be specially called to times of prayer. Maybe some people are gifted so that they can repeat their prayer lists all the time, but I'm not. Or maybe we've grown up with a distorted view of what prayer is. Do we approach prayer as a form of mental exercise—something that in our own natural power we can "do"? When we read Paul's imperative words, "pray without ceasing" (1 Thess. 5:17, NASB), we may come think of prayer as something meant only for super saints.

The fact is that Paul was addressing you and me— every one of us. God calls each of us pray continually. But we must realize this: before God calls us to prayer, He calls us to Himself. When God says, "Come away, my beloved"

(Song of Sol. 8:14a), He is calling every one of us. He is inviting you.

Second, we need to find a place to be entirely alone. Susanna Wesley, mother of John and Charles Wesley and more than a dozen other children, had absolutely no place to go inside her own home to get away from the children in order to be alone with the Lord. So when she pulled her apron up over her head, her children knew it was time to leave her alone. Most of us have better living circumstances than Susanna Wesley. If you have a bathroom, or even a large closet, you can find a place to be alone.

Third, we must learn what it takes to quiet our own spirit. Bombarded as we are by outside noise and information, we get totally out of touch with our own feelings and motives. Begin to be quiet by disconnecting from the ever-noisy TV and radio, and put limits on gab sessions with friends. Then you can take time to search your heart—with the help of the Holy Spirit—to find out what's really going on inside. Sometimes we don't really want to know what's going on in there. But you can't enter the secret place with God unless you enter as your true self. False fronts and masks will hinder you from experiencing God's presence. As David says in his great psalm of confession, only truth and honesty in the inward parts will allow us to enter where God abides (see Ps. 51:6).

Fourth, we need help prevent our minds from wandering. If you've ever tried to spend time alone with the Lord, you know what I mean. You manage to take a quiet break—but the minute you sit down, "the list" takes over your mind. You think, *I can't just sit here. There's wet laundry in the dryer, and I've got to pay this bill, and...and...and...* Failing to get anywhere spiritually, you give up.

For this reason, I recommend you enter into the secret place with God by meditating on His Word. I can think of no better way to corral and direct your straying thoughts than to guide them along the spiritual pathways of truth laid out by God's Spirit. And as you meditate on God's Word, God builds up your faith by revealing Himself to you. There in His Word, you can see Him at work; you can learn about His character. You can see Him act, loving and winning back the world, which includes you, to Himself.

Each of these four steps helps turn your heart toward God. Each step opens you up to the fifth thing that leads straight into the secret place—opening yourself to receive His love.

The need to be loved is the strongest need any of us possess. Most of our arguments and conflicts with other people have to do with the issue of being loved. Yet each of us has a huge void inside that the love of no human being can ever fill. Only God's love can fill it.

In order for God to fill us, our hearts must be wide open to Him—yielded to Him. Therefore, it's absolutely necessary that we learn to pray from our hearts. Praying from our heads, with our understanding, doesn't accomplish anything, because prayer is nothing more and nothing less than turning our hearts fully toward God, opening up all of what we are to Him, and in turn receiving His love in place of our emptiness.

This yielding is not something we do instinctively, and

most of us try too hard. What is it like to yield to Him? Consider Adam, just after he was created. There he was, a fine physical specimen made by God, perfect in every way. Yet there was no life in him. As Adam lay there on the ground, God bent down and breathed life into him. God is still doing that today, stopping to breathe life into our empty, needy souls. What did Adam do to receive this life? Nothing. He just lay there and let God do the breathing. In the same way, we must open ourselves to God, yield to Him, and simply allow Him to fill us.

Although I say "simply," that is difficult for our works-based mentality to grasp. We carry around long lists of the things we must do to be worthy enough to approach God. The Christian church has often added to this pressure, making us feel that we need to do more to please God so that He will be "happy" with us.

In actuality, all we are required to do is to relax and inhale the breath of the very Spirit of God, who is always present with us.

My Kingdom Is within You

Jesus promised the disciples that He would send the Holy Spirit so they wouldn't be left alone without Him after His death. He said, "You know him, for *he lives with you and will be in you*" (John 14:17b, emphasis added).

God Himself lives in you! His kingdom, the place where He rules and reigns, is inside of you.

You may have learned about prayer that storms the heavens to tear down strongholds (see 2 Cor. 10:4), and prayer that asks for our daily needs (see Matt. 6:11), but I'm talking about the kind of prayer that allows you to enter the kingdom of God. You can come right into God's presence. The Comforter lives right inside you, and He wants to give you peace.

This is an incredible fact—the kingdom of God is within you, and this makes God Himself accessible to you at any time.

I have studied the great women of faith down through the ages in order to understand how to enter into that secret place with God. God has helped women from every walk of life learn how to draw spiritual strength and courage from the kingdom within so that they could face the hard circumstances that surrounded them. Only in the secret place of prayer could they find inspiration for the dull and dry times, and comfort for the lonely and hurting times as well. These truly noble Christian women knew how to exhale their many worries and surrender their misconceptions about God that might have kept them from approaching Him. They understood what it meant to empty themselves of all worldly preoccupations that can fill up the inner rooms of our souls and push Him out. They also knew how to relax into, and breathe in, His very presence. They knew what it meant to inhale the peace that comes only from Him, like a spiritual fragrance. They knew how to pray, "Father, I want to meet with you in the secret place," and how to follow Him, day after day and year after year.

Prayer is as simple as breathing out and asking God to clear out the clutter and the noise within, asking Him to create that inner room where you can always go to meet with Him in secret.

Have you learned what it's like to have God's very presence fill you the way breath fills your lungs? You can easily enter into the secret place of your soul where God's Spirit dwells if you know the way.

The kind of prayer I am referring to is not about getting it right or about achieving a goal, the motivation for too many of our prayers; neither is it about making yourself presentable to God before you ask to meet with Him. There is a kind of intimate praying that can only come about as we learn to strip away pretense and come, just as we are, into the inner chamber with our Lord and King.

Some of us look at other Christian women, especially "prayer warriors" or "great women of faith" and think, *If only I knew how to pray the way she prays.* When we think this way, we are treating the subject of prayer as if we are going into another woman's home to see her decorating scheme, her lovely fabrics, furniture selection, and colors. We think, *If only I could deck myself out like her. If only I could come before God the way she does—then my life with God would take off and my prayers would become powerful.*

Prayer that brings us into intimate experiences with God does not involve imitating another or reproducing their prayers. You are your own person; you are unique. And there is a place of intimacy with you that God cannot find with anyone else. He wants you to have a relationship with Him that no one else can enjoy. Know this: *God wants you to be just exactly who you are.*

Many of us wish we were someone else. We want to enjoy God's presence, but we think, *God doesn't really want to meet with me.* Listen—you know what? God wants you to take yourself as you find yourself, and start from there. You can't change your history; you can't change mistakes or undo wrong things from your past. *You can't remake yourself into somebody you're not.* So begin with the person you are today. It's like standing in front of the mall-map sign that says You are here. God wants you to say, "God, I am here! Just as I am, I come."

Being able to enter into the deep love and peace of God in prayer is not about getting rid of flaws and faults. If it were, we would spend all our time trying to make ourselves perfect, and that never works. Entering your secret place requires nothing more than coming, for He says, "Everything and everyone that the Father has given me will come to me, and I won't turn any of them away" (John 6:37, CEV). Anytime, you can come as you are into the presence of the wonderful God who has said, "I am with you always..." (Matt. 28:20b).

What is the only requirement for finding your way to the secret place with God? Just begin. Begin by abandoning yourself to God, which means learning to rest in His divine presence no matter what your circumstances may be.

In abandoning yourself to God, you train your soul to rest in Him. You trust that He is in control of your life not only when everything goes well, but also when everything goes wrong. You learn to trust that He has not abandoned you and that He knows what's best for you when He allows different situations and circumstances into your life. You make a deliberate choice to believe that He is working something bigger into you than what you could accomplish by yourself.

I am not saying this is easy. It's not. But it works.

The Narrow Way

To find the peace of God that only He can give, we must abandon ourselves completely to Him. Abandonment is the key that unlocks the entry door into the secret place where our King and heavenly Bridegroom dwells.

In the secret place, God reveals His mysteries to us. He is our Bridegroom, and He longs to reveal His secrets to us, His bride. One of the greatest mysteries is the way God transforms us into people who bear the marks of Jesus Christ. Paul referred to this mystery when he wrote, "I bear on my body the marks of Jesus" (Gal. 6:17b). If we love and abandon ourselves to God, as Paul did, we will be transformed into His image.

Paul was describing Jesus' "narrow way" (see Matt. 7:13–14), a way that stands open before each one of us. Finding your way to this place in God requires giving Him the keys to everything: children, husband, family, home, possessions, friends, job, and dreams. We must place everything into His hands and leave it there for Him to do with as He sees fit.

What will it take to produce this kind of abandonment in us? It does not come easily, and it takes great faith. The greater our faith, the more we know God, and the better we know Him, the easier it will be to abandon ourselves freely without the slightest hesitation or holding back. What Jesus said is eternal truth: God is our center, and His kingdom is within us (see Luke 17:21).

The more we become completely united with Him in spirit, soul, and body (see 1 Thess. 5:23), the more the barriers of doubt, fear, and pride will melt in the warmth of His love. We will come into a place where peace, love, and eternal strength are ours because we are one with Him, peacefully resting in the wonder of His love.

Great Women of God Show Us the Way

Throughout history, great men and women alike have found their way into the secret place where God dwells. They have entered that place by learning the secrets of quiet prayer, and how to abandon themselves completely to God. They learned what it means to become His bride, and they were consumed with the love of God as they yielded themselves completely to His presence. In this book, we'll look at the lives of a few of these amazing women. From them, we can learn much about answering God's call to the secret place.

As we begin, I offer this prayer on your behalf:

Father, lead us out of the storms and stresses of life that distract us and keep us from knowing You. More than anything else, we want to know You. We want to open our hearts and our lives wide to You. Guide us by Your precious Holy Spirit to the secret place, where You can reveal Yourself in wonder, majesty, and holiness, in us and through us to a lost world. In Jesus' name, amen.

Chapter Two

✝

THE DEPTHS OF GOD

C ome up here!" the heavenly voice commanded (see Rev. 4:1b).

When Jesus Christ calls you into the secret place of prayer, it's an invitation like no other. That call from the depths of God's presence signals an unspeakable privilege, an open door to a revelation of God Himself. My one major goal in life is to be like the apostle John and to answer the call of God to come into the secret place. What about you?

In the book of Revelation, the veil is pulled back for a moment and we are afforded a glimpse of what John saw when he was called into the secret place. The apostle tells us: "On the Lord's Day I was in the Spirit, and I heard behind me a loud voice…" (Rev. 1:10).

When John turned to see who was calling, he was amazed. The One who commanded his attention was none other than Jesus. But it was not the Jesus he'd seen before— the itinerant Jewish rabbi in a robe and sandals. Here was the shining, resurrected Son of God, summoning John to come up with Him in the glorious heavenly sanctuary where He stood in the midst of fiery candlesticks. From His feet to His hair He was a blazing fire, so that "His face was like the sun shining in all its brilliance" (Rev. 1:16b).

John was so overcome by this shining revelation of God that he "fell at His feet like a dead man" (Rev. 1:17a, NASB). But Jesus placed His right hand on John and lifted him up—and went on to unfold one of the greatest revelations of God that anyone has ever received.

I don't expect to be another John, but I too want to meet with Jesus Christ in the secret and holy place where He dwells in Spirit and, like John, be taken into the depths of God. I want to be a vessel that reveals the awesome mysteries of God's grace and truth to the world. Is that the goal of your life too?

Battle and Blessing

The problem for most of us is that the busyness of life crowds out the time we could otherwise spend alone answering God's call. For example, one Sunday morning I was trying to find even ten minutes to be alone with God, but it seemed that it was not to be. I went into one room after another, and one of my children followed me wherever I went. At every step, I heard, "Mom, I need this," or "Can we do that?"

I was doing my best to see them merely as innocent children and I was trying to maintain a good attitude, but I felt bombarded. I kept thinking, *Why is it such a battle to get to the blessing?*

Interestingly, I've learned that God is not absent from

such circumstances. In fact, God is actually very present in these circumstances, allowing them to happen for a reason. As we're being pressed, he grants us an opportunity to see ourselves as we really are. Far from setting up these situations to hurt us or keep us away from Himself, He allows such circumstances to help us see aspects of ourselves that we would otherwise miss. We don't necessarily enjoy that. Our human natures aren't eager to be exposed to His light, but that's the first step toward transformation. He is allowing us to see (through trial and testing) our need for His help.

Besides, God is God. It makes no difference what circumstances surround us; He can still meet with us, and He can still provide for our every need.

I am writing this to you, not because I merely *hope* that it's true or because it sounds like the spiritual thing to say. I'm writing to tell you, as one who has received the true grace of God, that there is a way into the secret place where He dwells—*even in the midst of whatever kind of bombardment or fiery furnace you are going through.* The way is not to try to escape the flames, but to go through them.

Let me tell you how I learned this truth.

My Own Personal Fire

God made sure that I could learn, in the midst of the hot flames of testing around me, to walk in the burning presence of God. He showed me things that I hadn't understood before—events from the past that were hurtful to me; times when I felt spiritually dry; and long stretches in which I had felt alone, forgotten, left out, and overlooked. He redeemed those times by showing me that, from His perspective, I have never been apart from His great love for me. He has brought me out of the unpleasant place where I felt stuck for many years.

For years I was at home all the time, and everyone knew me only as "Jim Goll's wife" or "the pastor's wife." Sometimes it's difficult to live with a person who is really well-known and liked. (For some people, that person may be a parent or sibling, or a coworker.) I think it's the most difficult to be left behind as the one who's holding down the fort.

People would call our home and say, "Oh, you have the most wonderful husband. His meetings are so awesome, and he is so anointed. You must feel so blessed to be married to him."

While I agreed with them that, yes, James is an awesome vessel of God's grace and truth, something in my heart wanted to say, *But what about me? Where is the affirmation I need to feel valued for my contribution to 'our' ministry?* I felt like an appendage. I could try to be "more spiritual" and want to please only God. Yet, honestly I had to admit that I, like anyone else, wanted to be known and to feel valued and respected for my labors.

What made it worse in those early years was our desperate desire to have children, but we were unable to conceive. I was barren for seven years, but then God dramatically and miraculously touched and healed me. I was absolutely ecstatic and filled with indescribable wonder and thanksgiving.

My pregnancy with Justin, our oldest, went well, except for some mild morning sickness in the early months. Then, during my second pregnancy with our daughter, GraceAnn, I became very, very ill. I spent months lying in bed. I was too sick and weak to even hold up my Bible because it was too heavy. I couldn't eat anything; I could barely keep down a tablespoon of liquid at a time. I looked terminally ill. It was truly by the grace of God that GraceAnn was born a totally healthy baby, weighing nine pounds, six ounces.

But my body was so depleted. Shortly thereafter, I became pregnant with our son Tyler. Again I became very ill, not quite as bad but serious enough that I lay in bed for months. My stomach seemed to be over generating digestive juices that were eating me up from the inside out.

And so it went through the pregnancies for three of our four children. I was left alone all day, except for my babies and toddlers. I didn't see or talk to other adults. I didn't watch TV or listen to the radio. I couldn't read anything because I couldn't hold up a book. All I did was take care of little children, rest, and hope in God.

That's how things became clear spiritually. God visited me in quiet ways during those long days. With no other distractions in the way, God began to speak to me, connecting the dots of my life, so to speak. I didn't know it then, but there was more testing ahead.

While we were living in Kansas City where James was serving on a church staff, we entered into a season of unusual spiritual warfare. Suddenly one morning, James got incredibly sick. I found him delirious, hallucinating in our bedroom. I rushed him to the doctor, but for two weeks the doctor could not figure out what was going on.

Almost as soon as James pulled through, I got slammed. In the midst of this, we were trying to sell our home (without a realtor). Suddenly, I became severely ill with a dangerously high temperature. I kept on showing the house to potential buyers, working constantly to keep it perfectly clean and taking care of my small children. After a few weeks of this frantic pace, I started to realize that there were periods of time I could not account for. My temperature was so high that I was blacking out.

That was when my doctor said, "Okay, let's put you in the hospital."

After I was admitted to the hospital, things got worse. They put me in an isolation room where everyone who came to see me was required to wear a mask. The physicians started asking me the most bizarre questions. What kind of sexual relations had I had? What was my lifestyle like? Nothing was sacred, and I felt completely humiliated—stripped down to my very soul.

My lowest point came when my doctor stood at the head of my bed rattling off to himself a list of deadly diseases that I might have. Bewildered with my symptoms, he was saying, "Well now, if it's cancer we can expect to see this symptom..." He went on to catalog just about every terrible life-threatening disease I'd ever heard of. Then he walked out without reaching a diagnosis.

My kids had been farmed out to friends and family. They were able to visit me a few times, but the masks and robes produced a fearful experience for them. I longed to see them and hold them but wasn't sure what this experience was doing to them. On his own, my husband was trying to sell our home, while his wife was lying in the hospital bed, still sick as a dog. Not to mention miserable, scared, empty, and feeling totally alone.

I have to say that no spiritual enlightenment came my way in the long hours of that dark night. I heard no comforting statements from God's throne room like, *Yes, I am with you, Ann,* to carry me through, at any time during those long days. I felt numb spiritually and mentally, as though I had taken my head off my shoulders. I couldn't think or try to process anything. I remembered that God had promised He would always be with me, but I couldn't feel Him, hear Him, or sense His presence.

The Fire Bride

Through that terrible ordeal I learned what treasure can be deposited within us as we pass through the fire—when we keep our hearts open to God and to His deeper workings in our lives. Some of us think that God's greatest goal is to make everything easy and comfortable for us. While it's true that He wants to bless us with good things, He desires something else even more. He yearns for deep friendship with us. He longs for true intimacy.

Intimacy with God…hmm…sounds romantic, doesn't it? But our God is holy and His holiness is a consuming fire (see Deut. 4:24). He draws us closer to Himself by kindling a fire that draws us like moths out of the darkness toward its great light. Drawn by a force that's beyond ourselves, we come closer.

As we get closer, the fire of God begins to make us uncomfortable. The light of His holiness begins to scorch the dross and the chaff within us. We experience turmoil as we become painfully aware of our sins, shortcomings, and unworthiness to be in His beautiful, holy presence. We become painfully aware that we have become idolaters, nurturing false passions of our soul and flesh, and that our idols have kept us trapped in worldliness.

Our turmoil grows deeper and stronger until it becomes a battle over our very souls. We long for Him and we remember the seal of the Holy Spirit, like the engagement ring pledged as a promise of a coming wedding day (see Eph. 4:30). Yet at the same time we are overwhelmed with our failings, angers, jealousies, and lusts. Within, we cry out, *How could He possibly love me or want me as I am?*

Oh, but our heavenly Lover already sees and knows everything. Fully aware of our every fault, He nevertheless calls us to Himself. Unfortunately, our sense of unworthiness causes us to resist Him and hold back from running into His arms with abandonment.

Eventually, we discover that there is only one thing to do. In the moment of our greatest soul agony, when we feel ourselves to be the most useless and unworthy in His eyes, we must run to Him and cry out, "Help me, my Lord and my God!" But there in His wonderful, gracious embrace, He will cover all our weaknesses, needs, and soul sickness.

Rushing toward Him, the wind of our desperation fuels the flame of His passion, which burns away our dross and chaff with consuming love. In this moment we begin to understand why He has allowed all the mistakes, sins, failures, and disappointments.

These lines from Frances Thompson's famous poem "The Hound of Heaven" echo the voice of God, revealing a great mystery of His wonderful ways:

> All which I took from thee I did but take,
> Not for thy harms,
> But just that thou might'st seek it in My arms.
> All which thy child's mistake
> Fancies as lost, I have stored for thee at home:
> Rise, clasp My hand, and come!

Why do we wait so long? We yearn for the fire of our Lover, but we're afraid to run into His arms, knowing He is a "living flame of love," as John of the Cross called Him. We are afraid of the process it takes to fully embrace Him and be caught up in Him forever.

So we hang onto our worldly passions, interests, positions, power, possessions, people—all in an attempt to anchor ourselves here on earth, where we feel a little more secure. We worry, *What will He ask of me? What will He force me to give up?* We attempt to bargain our way out of our perceived losses. *What will He let me keep?* Sometimes we fall into condemnation because we know we should not consider earthly "treasures" to be more valuable than God Himself.

Instead of being consumed by the blissful joy of godly passion and the ecstasy of spiritual freedom, we are consumed by guilt. Even our hesitancy reinforces our false belief that we don't "qualify" for His love. Now hopelessness and new turmoil begin to pull us down.

Sooner or later, we look up. Who is this Man standing before us? It's Jesus, the living, loving Son of God! God Himself in the flesh captures us with the intense look of love in His eyes. His heart calls us tenderly, *Just let go of your struggle. This minute. Let it go...and come to Me!*

What am I waiting for? we ask. Letting go of all fear and resistance, we run headlong into His arms. Instantly, the Holy Spirit breathes upon the embers of our smoldering passion, setting our hearts ablaze with love for Him.

At last—the Fire Bride of God!

Where she once feared the fire, to her own delighted amazement she now cries out for more. *More fire!* The intensity of heat that tried her heart has transformed it into precious, purified gold. She is complete in Him and her heart will never again be polluted by other, lesser loves. Her heart is no longer hers; it now belongs to Him.

Worth Everything

To finish my story, the doctors finally discovered that I had severe pneumonia and eventually were able to bring it under control. I went home to convalesce, and in time I was well again.

In the midst of all the upheaval of that terrible time, what I had needed the most I had received directly from God Himself—healing for my soul. Now I could see God's hand in all that we had endured.

Some weeks later, I had a dream. In it, an angel came to me and hit me on the head. When he struck me, my skull opened and the light of God radiated inside me. It was 4:00

a.m., and I sat bolt upright in bed, charged with a supernatural energy from this encounter with God. In this moment of illumination, I saw clearly that God is utterly faithful to be with us at all times and through all things. Even when we allow other loves and circumstances to blind us to Him, He is still there, longing to love and be loved.

Something else broke my heart. He is truly the only heavenly Lover, the sole One who has the right to our hearts. He created our hearts, and no other being in this universe will be as faithful as He is. His love is all-encompassing. How can we ignore it for another moment?

Healing for Our Souls

Most of us think "salvation" is only about getting saved from hell so we can go to heaven. But salvation is about so much more than that. Jesus opened the way for us to come into the very presence of God so that our souls, which were wounded in the Fall, might be healed and restored to wholeness. We can never be whole without God. Until we rejoin ourselves to Him, we will always have a soul wound in the place where He should be.

If we do not overcome our fear of His fire and return to His side to be made whole, we will forever be filled with that deep, empty longing for something to fill that wound. We will never fill it with what the world has to offer, no matter how much we try. The only solution is to abandon ourselves to Him so that He can rejoin Himself to us by the power of His Holy Spirit in us.

Companions for the Journey

As I have learned the way to the secret place with God, I am thankful that I've found spiritual companions to show me the way, spiritually minded men and women who have gone through the fire themselves and have come out purified and filled with a desire to share the grace they have received, wanting to share it with others by means of their writings.

What I have learned about entering the secret place with God is by no means the final word on the subject. In the next chapters, we will gain more insights regarding deep and fulfilling intimacy with God from some great women of the Christian faith, including Madame Jeanne Guyon, St. Teresa of Avila, Susanna Wesley, Fanny Crosby, Basilea Schlink, Gwen Shaw, and Elizabeth Alves.

From these women, each of whom has passed through the fire, we can receive a wealth of rich insight and heavenly blessing. However, before we begin I want to offer two words of direction.

First, their lives are to be used only as way markers. They can help you see where you might be on your own journey. The principles they learned and taught do not lay out a "step-by-step" list of dos and don'ts for entering into God's presence. They do not present a "canned" or legalistic approach to spiritual growth.

Second, let these stories help sharpen your spiritual focus so that all your attention is directed toward God and God alone. Be aware of the subtle temptation to take your eyes off Him and look at your struggles, or to forget His infinite ability by focusing on your own limited abilities. It's all about Him, not you.

All About Him

The life we are called to live, hidden and kept in the deep love of God, is not about us at all. It is about learning that we can trust Him utterly and abandon ourselves to Him completely. We can place all that concerns us into His care and learn to follow Him wherever He sees fit to lead us. He will take care of our every need, show us how to live in His kingdom, and use us however He desires to do so.

Are you ready to begin this journey? Daunting as it may sound, I urge you not to be afraid. Don't hesitate. God is your matchless Bridegroom who wants to join Himself to you in spirit. He has chosen you just as much as He has chosen me or any of the women profiled in this book. He longs to give us His Spirit, His beauty, and His grace, to infuse us with His very own eternal nature.

Father, thank You that Your salvation is full and complete for both now and eternity. Through the wisdom of those who have walked this way before us and through your Holy Spirit present deep within, heal my wounds. Fill the emptiness deep inside my soul that drives me to seek comfort and satisfaction in everything except You. Open my eyes, Lord, as you opened the eyes of these great women of the faith who have gone before us. Let me see You and You alone. In Jesus' name I pray, amen.

Part Two

Pilgrims of the Secret Place

Chapter Three

———+———

Jeanne Guyon (1648–1717)

CALLED
DEEPER STILL

Does God have "favorites"? Sometimes we think so, but the truth is that God's call to spiritual intimacy comes to many—and only a few respond. Why is this? Is it because we instinctively know there is a cost to be paid if we want to enter into deeper mysteries of God?

One person who was willing to pay the price of spiritual intimacy with God was Madame Jeanne Guyon, a French woman born into a wealthy Roman Catholic family in the 1600s. As a result of her amazing experiences in prayer, she wrote several books, which have become known as some the greatest writings in all of Christian history, by now translated into many languages around the world.

Her writings have given me both courage and comfort, because I can identify with her struggles, which led her into extraordinary experiences in God. She asked the questions I have asked: *Why did God allow that to happen in my life? Why am I so restless, and longing for more of God?*

Madame Guyon intrigues me not because she offers spiritual formulas (which she does not), but because she gives us a glimpse of the deeper work God does inside us when we become fully yielded to Him. In this journey to the secret place, Jeanne Guyon is almost a one-of-a-kind guide. Although she was an everyday woman of her time, she entered into the depths of God, and then enabled others to find their way in the Spirit as well.

Her wisdom provides us with a truly unique spiritual perspective. Her words and experiences lift us up to a higher spiritual realm. They allow us to soar like birds riding the winds of an upward-sweeping breeze, to a higher place in spirit. Her insights enable us to assess the places in our spiritual journey that can wound us badly and throw so many of us off course spiritually. Once we adopt her wise viewpoint for ourselves, we can begin to see in a new light the outlines of our path with our great heavenly Lover.

This is not just high-sounding spiritual talk. The wisdom I have gained from Madame Guyon's life has helped me to understand why difficult things have happened in my life and in the lives of my children. Her godly wisdom has helped guide their lives and has matured me into a more godly mother. To me that kind of spiritual growth is more precious than gold.

Amazingly, it was never Madame Guyon's intent to write a book of any kind. In the Catholic faith there are men and women known as spiritual directors, people who are responsible for the spiritual growth of anyone who is serious about faith and who wants their guidance. Jeanne would go to her spiritual directors and pose all her questions. The main reason we have her writings is because her spiritual directors commanded her to write about her spiritual experiences and insights as a matter of obedience. Then, ironic as it may seem, what she had written raised suspicion in Church officials and she was jailed as a possible heretic.

Madame Guyon's most profound insights came to us from a cold, dirty stone-walled prison cell where she wrote in defense of the one belief upon which her faith rested— that entering in unity with God happens only as we abandon ourselves totally to Him.

As she put it, "you [must become] fully convinced that it is on the nothing in man that God establishes His greatest works....He destroys that He might build. For when He is about to rear His sacred temple in us, He first totally razes that vain and pompous edifice that human art and power had erected. And from its horrible ruins, a new structure is formed, by His power only."[1]

This was the heart of Madame Guyon, filled with a faith that was rich, strong, alive, and unbeatable, no matter what rose up against her. The true story of her life is better than any fictional tale.

Beginnings

Jeanne Guyon was born prematurely on April 18, 1648, in the eighth month of her mother's pregnancy. Infant mortality rates were high in those days, and the baby girl was suspended between life and death for some time. Little Jeanne's health remained touch and go until she was almost three years old. Unfortunately, frail health would plague her the rest of her life.

Jeanne's father was wealthy and influential, and could have paid for childcare help in their home. But her mother was something of an enigma and opted to send her tiny, sick baby to a convent where Ursuline nuns would care for her for several months. Perhaps her mother had lived too long under the emotional fallout of so many infant deaths. When little Jeanne was returned to her parents, her mother's heart had cooled toward her sickly daughter and had embraced Jeanne's older brother instead. Jeanne became a neglected child. In her memoirs, she recalls that her mother spent little time with her and seemed to count her of little value. She was left entirely to the care of the household servants.

On the other hand, Jeanne's father loved her dearly. When he saw his wife neglecting their daughter, he arranged to send her to another convent where she might receive better care. So from the age of four until she was seven, she lived at a convent of Benedictine sisters.

Jeanne's life with the sisters left a lasting imprint. Living there in the convent and attending church services every day, Jeanne grew to love hearing about God, being in church, and being dressed in religious garb. Convent life planted seeds deeply in Jeanne's heart. From an early age, she became hungry for God.

In fact, she became unusually spiritually sensitive. As a

little child, one night she dreamed of hell and cried out, "Oh my God, if you will have mercy on me and spare me yet a little longer I will never more offend you."[2]

Jeanne returned home briefly, but it seemed that her heart would never find a home in any earthly place. Her mother's rejection caused her to ignore Jeanne when she was ill, which was much of the time. Once she almost died of a sudden hemorrhage.

Soon, Jeanne's father sent her to another convent run by Benedictines. Then she was moved to yet another convent, and allowed only brief visits home. When she was almost ten years of age, her father brought her home again until a nun of the order of St. Dominica, a close family friend, persuaded him to permit Jeanne to live with her at her convent. But her care was not good. In time, her father discovered that his daughter had become emaciated, and he brought her home.

At age eleven, Jeanne was sent again to the Ursulines, this time under the care of a half sister who also lived with the nuns. This young woman was very nurturing, and Jeanne's spirit flourished under her care. Jeanne grew in her love and devotion to God by leaps and bounds. Later, she once again returned home.

(Now all this shuttling in and out of convents and sending children away sounds terrible to us today. But keep in mind that it was a common practice in those days for people of means to allow their children to be brought up by monks or nuns.)

For Jeanne there was lasting benefit, because away from

her mother, immersed in the holy atmosphere of these cloisters, Jeanne felt her first touches from God. What was this deep stirring she felt inside, this sense of someone calling her? Having no instruction about a personal relationship with God through Christ, Jeanne could only feel her way through institutional Christianity. She went regularly to confession, as was the Catholic custom, and she loved prayer. Even as a child she experienced a desire to suffer martyrdom; she and the other girls living at the convent would act out scenes in which they would take turns playing the role of martyr.

Though Jeanne would never go to a hostile foreign mission field or suffer physical martyrdom, she was in fact destined to suffer, not only from her unexplained illnesses, but from a kind of living death at the hands of those in authority over her.

Soul in Turmoil

When Jeanne returned home for the last time, nothing had changed in her mother's heart; if anything, it became even harder toward the little girl. She devoted most of her attentions to Jeanne's brother, whom she allowed to be absolutely brutal toward Jeanne at times. One time he threw her from the top of a coach, badly bruising her. He often beat her. If Jeanne had something he wanted, it was taken from her and given to him. In their mother's eyes, he could do no wrong and Jeanne could do no right. As for Jeanne's care, it was mostly left to a servant girl who was allowed to beat the girl and treat her with total contempt. In fact, all the servants, if they wanted to be in good standing with her mother, would report every little "infraction."

To help Jeanne stand up under such unrelenting oppression, at that time all she had to hold onto spiritually were the written prayers in her Catholic prayer book. No one had told her that you could talk to God in your own words. Nevertheless, in moments of despair Jeanne began to cling to God, though He seemed distant.

Suddenly, at about thirteen years of age, Jeanne transformed physically. She was quite tall for her age and blossomed into a very pretty young woman. Suddenly, too, her mother seemed to like her more. She fussed and primped with Jeanne's hair and clothes, took her to parties and social events, and even took her traveling abroad. It became quite apparent that she was very proud of Jeanne's physical beauty.

All of this attention produced in Jeanne pride and vanity. In a way, who could blame her, after having been rejected for so long? However, there remained in her heart a strange tug—a sense that someone was calling to her. At one time a cousin who was on his way to a mission in China came to visit. Something in this young man—perhaps a certain spiritual fire or a single-hearted purity—spoke deeply to Jeanne, reawakening her earlier desire for God.

She passed the next years of her life, from twelve to fifteen, feeling torn inside. On the surface she dressed in fine clothes, but underneath her spirit was drawn away from the fine things of the world toward an upward calling. By reading spiritual works, such as the writings of St. Frances DeSales, Jeanne's soul deepened. Eventually, she began to spend more time with her prayer book; she was still trying to connect with that distant, elusive voice that seemed to call out to her.

The streets were full of beggars, destitute widows, and orphans; Jeanne gave all she had to the poor. Gathering a small group of poor people together, she taught the catechism. When her parents were not at home, for her mother would have loudly disapproved, she invited the poor in to eat with her, serving them with great respect.

Alone

During this time, Jeanne discovered the writings of a woman known as Madame de Chantel. Never before had she heard anyone speak of the things this woman of faith talked about—especially something she called "mental prayer," praying to God freely from the heart. According to Madame de Chantel, it was the beginning of the way into the secret place of union with God.

Something in Jeanne's young heart leaped.

However, when Jeanne asked her confessor to teach her this kind of prayer, he refused. Pray without a prayer book? He was aghast. How ridiculous! Unspiritual! Perhaps even dangerous! She should stick to the known paths. What did it matter, he said flatly, if written prayers were boring and lifeless to her? Who did she think she was to even consider other methods of prayer?

But Jeanne's heart was burning. She continued to fight in bouts with pride and vanity, and each round drove her all the more toward the desire for spiritual freedom. What if it were really possible to know God personally and experience Him intimately, as Madame de Chantel suggested?

She begged a community of nuns to take her in, but, knowing that her father would disapprove, they refused her. So, with no one to guide her, no one she could trust to lead her on her spiritual quest, Jeanne forged ahead on her own.

Teach me how to know You, Lord! her heart cried.

She had no way of knowing where that prayer would lead.

At this same time, Jeanne's family traveled to Paris. At first, her heart was nearly overwhelmed by the whirl of social engagements, beautiful clothes, jewelry, and perfumes. Handsome suitors flocked to her door. The romantic novels Jeanne occasionally read only added to her increasing vanity. Several advantageous offers of marriage came, but they were rejected by her father.

Eventually, one wealthy and influential suitor did get through to Jeanne's father. One day a servant approached Jeanne with a document to sign. "Sign quickly, please! It's for your father." Taking up a quill, Jeanne inked her name… not realizing that with each letter she scratched onto the paper she was signing herself away on formal "articles of marriage." She was just fifteen years old.

Two days before she was to be married, Jeanne saw her suitor for the first time. Her already turbulent young spirit sank into deep depression. Of her wedding day she would later write, "No sooner was I at the house of my new spouse than I perceived it would be for me a house of mourning."[3]

Immediately, it was also apparent that Jeanne's new mother-in-law despised her. She wrote:

At my father's house we were obliged to behave in a genteel way and to speak with propriety. All that I said was applauded. Here, they never listened to me except to contradict and find fault. If I spoke well, they said it was to give them a lesson. If any questions were started at my father's, he encouraged me to speak freely. Here, if I spoke my sentiments they said it was to enter into a dispute. They put me to silence in an abrupt and shameful manner and scolded me from morning until night....My mother-in-law conceived such a desire to oppose me in everything. And in order to vex me, she made me perform the most humiliating offices. Her disposition was so extraordinary....I was made the victim of her humors. All her occupation was to thwart me.[4]

Not only did this bitter old woman despise Jeanne, she turned the heart of her son, Jeanne's new husband, against her also: "[My mother-in-law] inspired the like sentiments in her son. And so they would make people who were my inferiors take place above me."[5]

Sadly, Jeanne found no support or comfort from her own family. She wrote, "My mother, who had a high sense of honor, could not endure that. When she heard [about my dishonor] from others—for I told her nothing—she chided me, thinking I did it because I didn't know how to keep my rank and had no spirit. And so I dared not tell her how it was, but I was almost ready to die with the agonies of grief and continual vexation.

"What made it worse," Jeanne continued, "was that my mother related to my mother-in-law the pains I had caused her from infancy. They then reproached me saying I was a challenging and an evil spirit. My husband made me stay all day long in my mother-in-law's room without any liberty of retiring into my own apartment. She spoke disadvantageously of me to everyone, to lessen the affection and esteem that some had entertained for me.

"She galled me with the grossest affronts before the finest company. [In this way] she found the secret of extinguishing my vivacity, and rendering me stupid. Some of my former acquaintances hardly knew me. Those who had not seen me before said, 'Is this the person famed for such abundance of wit? She can't say two words. She is a fine picture!'"[6]

Poor Jeanne, just sixteen years old, was driven to despair. Her spirit was dying, and in agony she wrote, "I had no one to confide in who might share my affliction and assist me to bear it....I resolved to have no confidant. It was not from any natural cruelty that my husband treated me [badly]. He loved me passionately, but was ardent and hasty, and my mother-in-law continually irritated him about me."[7]

In this horrible crucible of affliction, she began to cry out to God—not in the standard formal prayers that she had been taught by the Roman Catholic Church, but from the depths of her being.

"It was in a condition so deplorable, oh my God, that I began to perceive the need I had of Your assistance. This situation was perilous to me. I met with none but admirers abroad, those who flattered me to my hurt. It was to be feared, lest at such a tender age, amid all the strange domestic crosses I had to bear, I might be drawn away. But You, by Your goodness and love, gave it quite another turn.

"By these re-doubled strokes you did draw me to Yourself and by Your crosses effected what Your caresses could not effect. Not only this, You made use of my natural pride to keep me within the limits of my duty."[8]

Finding the Door

More time would pass before Jeanne made the discovery that turned all her sufferings into spiritual gold. At age sixteen, she had her first child, a son, and at nineteen, her second son was born. Both pregnancies wore her down physically, while her family continued to grind away at her spirit. Her only moments of solace were those times when she was alone crying out to God to help her.

Shortly after the birth of her second child, she met a man from the Order of St. Francis. He had lived in solitude for five years, caught up in the love of God, and had just emerged from this long retreat with a kind of glow about him that was unearthly. Jeanne's father, knowing her devotion to God, arranged for her to meet with him.

There in the serene peace of a monastery, away from the glare and abuse of her mother-in-law and husband, Jeanne found it difficult to contain herself. Question after question poured out from her hungry heart. The kindly brother listened with patience, not so much to her, but as though he were listening to another voice. When she finished, he lifted his face to hers and stared into her eyes.

"You must accustom yourself, Madame, to seek God in your heart, and you will there find Him. For"—and he quoted the words of Jesus Christ—"'The kingdom of God cometh not with observation....the kingdom of God is within you'" (Luke 17:20–21, KJV).[9]

A door to a whole new world was opened to Jeanne. The light of revelation flooded in, and she became illuminated with understanding. She realized that God was not only "out there" somewhere; the God who transcends time and space dwelled in a secret place within her. What was even more stunning was the other truth that flooded her soul at the same time. She realized, *If God is in me, then nothing can separate us. Nothing can come between God's love and me.*

Suddenly, nothing was easier for her than prayer. Hours flew by like moments—and the joy and intensity of her devotion increased. As she put it, "The fervency of my love allowed me no intermission."[10]

Now, she was able to bear the ill treatment of her husband and mother-in-law, no matter how insulting or rigorous, silently and without inner tumult. She was swept away from the cares of the world around her, having found that place inside where she could go and meet with God. Within her own soul at all times, she could retreat to a secret and holy place where she could spend time with Him.

In time, Jeanne became so attuned to God's presence that she scarcely knew what she was eating. Occasionally she missed what people were saying to her, and she went for long periods without speaking. You might think such great devotion to God would earn her the admiration of her family and of the religious community, but nothing was further from the truth.

More Opposition

Jeanne's husband became jealous of her devotion to God. Her confessor, who had previously called Jeanne a "saint," began to publicly speak against her. She had privately confided in him about her experience, and he betrayed her by spreading the word that she was under a delusion. This whole idea of meeting with God—sheer insanity!

When Jeanne's family learned about her new devotion, they led the charge. She was persecuted from all sides and forbidden to pray. They went so far as to check on her every thirty minutes to interrupt her if she was in prayer. At one point, her husband refused to let her go outdoors, because he wanted to keep her where someone could watch and control her every waking moment.

But Jeanne's understanding of prayer was far deeper than they understood. It transcended words. She now understood that true prayer is resting in the real presence of God. This revelation was so deeply embedded in her spirit that she could not stop praying. To be conscious was to be in God's living presence, with a deep abiding awareness of His strength, peace, and comfort. As a result, simply the look on her face radiated the presence of God, which infuriated her family all the more.

Just when Jeanne thought she had come through the worst of the fire, she experienced new suffering in ways she never could have imagined. Shortly after the birth of Jeanne's third child, a daughter, a terrifying plague of smallpox ripped through France. Her little girl and oldest son became feverish. Though Jeanne's husband wanted to take her and their younger son away to protect them, her mother-in-law refused to allow it.

To contract smallpox was to receive a virtual death sentence, and now Jeanne found herself and all three of her children stuck in this fatal trap. Fear for herself and for her children warred against her soul, threatening to tear her away from her internal place of peace with God.

Jeanne found herself in the battle of her life. When she turned her eyes and her spirit inward, there she found her heavenly King ruling all things in serene order. Nothing was beyond His control. But when she turned her attention outward to her flushed and fevered children calling piteously for water and for comfort, her mother's heart was ripped in two.

At this moment Jeanne knew that God was calling her, once and for all, to abandon the whole world and enter into the depths of love with Him alone.

Only by an act of sheer will did Jeanne make her choice. She would take her fear of loss and death to the cross and allow this part of herself to die. She knew that only in this way could she experience the peace that comes when there is nothing left to stand between God and herself.

Jeanne wrote later about how she sacrificed herself to divine providence. Almost at once, Jeanne felt the symptoms of smallpox coming on. When she told her husband, he brushed it off as "just your imagination." But within hours,

Jeanne was doubled over with intense stomach pain, a splitting headache, and a high fever. Still her family refused to believe she was ill. Her lungs became inflamed, and she was left gasping for breath and denied proper treatment because her mother-in-law refused to send for a doctor.

Divine providence alone came to her aid. A doctor who had treated her in the past felt moved for no apparent reason to pay a call and see if Jeanne was well. She wrote, "Never was a man more surprised when he saw the condition I was in. The smallpox, which could not come out, had fallen on my nose with such force that it was quite black. He thought it was gangrened and was going to fall off. My eyes were like two coals...."[11]

The surgeon was appalled. At once, he railed at the mother-in-law for her gross negligence, only to hear her insist that he leave Jeanne alone and untreated. But while they argued, Jeanne felt only tremendous peace deep within.

"I was not alarmed....For I longed to make a sacrifice of all things and was pleased that God would avenge Himself on that face which had [in the past] betrayed me into so much faithlessness."[12]

When the doctor returned, against the mother-in-law's objections, he bled Jeanne at once. (Bleeding was the means of treating most major illnesses in those times.) Jeanne wrote, "Though the smallpox came out immediately, I am more inclined to show how advantageous it is to resign oneself to God without reserve. For though in appearance He leaves us for a time, it is only to prove and exercise our faith. He never fails us when our need of Him is the more pressing."[13]

This was not the end of her terrible ordeal. "The blackness and swelling of my nose went away, and I believe had they continued to bleed me, I would have felt better, but for want of that I grew worse again. The malady fell into my eyes and inflamed them with such severe pain that I thought I should lose them both. I had violent pains for three weeks. I could not shut my eyes; they were so full of the smallpox, nor open them by reason of the pain. My throat, palate, and gums were likewise so filled with the pox that I could not swallow broth or take nourishment without suffering extremely. My whole body looked leprous. All who saw me said that they had never seen such a shocking spectacle.

"But," she continued, "as to my soul, it was kept in a contentment that cannot be expressed. The hopes of its liberty, by the loss of that beauty, which had so frequently brought me under bondage, rendered me so satisfied and so united to God, that I would not have changed my condition for that of the most happy prince in the world."[14]

The unshakable peace of her abandonment to God would sustain Jeanne through a painful loss. For though her daughter and older son survived, her younger son succumbed to the ravages of the disease.

Following her illness, Jeanne's face and body were hideously scarred. Her husband, horrified that his wife had lost her physical beauty, forced her to use an ointment "to recover [her] complexion and to fill up the hollows of the smallpox." She writes, "I had seen wonderful effects from it upon others, and therefore at first had a mind to try them. But jealous of God's work, I would not allow it. There was a voice in my heart that said, 'If I would have had you fair, I would have left you as you were.'"[15]

Jeanne was moving deeper into her ability to trust divine providence alone. And her next move was, in a way, a declaration that she would, from now on, follow God alone. She wrote that, because of her devotion to God, and against her husband's wishes, "I was obliged to lay aside every remedy, and to go into the air which made the pitting worse, to expose myself in the street when the redness of the smallpox was at its worse, in order to make my humiliation triumph where I had exalted my pride."[16]

Jeanne was moving into depths of God that few people enter, though the way lies open to us all.

Total Abandonment to God

About a year later, Jeanne's daughter died of another illness. In short order, she bore two more children. Not long afterward, Jeanne's husband became very ill, and it soon became apparent he was dying. Despite all the abuses he had heaped on her for years and years, as he lay on his deathbed she went to him and asked, "If there is anything I have ever done to hurt or to wound you—will you forgive me?"

Some hardness in her husband's heart must have broken, because he could only stare at her in disbelief. "No," he said. "You did me no wrong. I did not deserve you."[17]

You may well think that after her husband's death, life got better for Jeanne. Instead, it got worse. For years, she continued to try to find a confessor who could understand and support her. Instead, she was assigned to spiritual leaders who disliked or distrusted her, men who were caught up in the political jockeying that often went on between the religious orders of the day. Some were even jealous of her, because wherever she went, word of her holiness and great devotion spread. People were drawn to her and tried to seek her out, though all she wanted was to live a life withdrawn from the world so she could remain caught up in the constant love of God.

It was through a "providential" meeting that Jeanne met the one man in all of France who seemed to understand her. A Barnabite friar, François LaCombe, not only believed in Jeanne's spiritual wisdom, but also encouraged her to write a small book, which was published in 1685 under the title *A Short and Easy Method of Prayer*. This small work would ignite the hearts of devout men and women throughout Europe and become her most important writing, a true spiritual classic.

And it would also bring about persecution that lasted virtually for the rest of Jeanne's life. In fact, Lacombe—the one true friend she found in her lifetime—was imprisoned by the church for promoting her "heresy." He died two years after her book was published.

In 1688, at forty years of age, Jeanne also was imprisoned. It was there she was forced by spiritual directors to write more. As she wrote, she knew that every word and every phrase would be dissected by heresy hunters in the church and quite likely used against her. It was only by the intervention of Louis XIV's second wife, Madame Maintenon, that her life was spared and she was released.

Finally, Jeanne was allowed to live out the final years of her life in the solitude and peace with God she had craved throughout her entire life. On June 9, 1717, Jeanne Guyon found her way from the shackles of her earthly existence into the loving arms of her beloved heavenly Bridegroom. At long last, she was totally abandoned to the love of God.

Jeanne Guyon's Legacy

To this day, Madame Jeanne Guyon's writings are considered to be among the most powerful and pure Christian writings penned by any woman in history. Great Christian leaders such as John Wesley, Count Zinzendorf, Hudson Taylor, Jessie Penn-Lewis, and Watchman Nee considered this unassuming French woman as one of their true spiritual guides.

Through her life of utter devotion, countless Christians have been taught how to find their own way into the secret place where God abides—within.

Although Madame Guyon did not have the benefit of understanding spiritual warfare or intercession and may have therefore suffered some things unnecessarily, it is clear that the difficulties she suffered were allowed by God to train her in deeper faith. Although she may have overemphasized suffering and embraced martyrdom in an unbalanced way, especially in her younger days, given the culture and times in which she lived, we can easily overlook these imbalances for the gold that is in her writings.

Lessons Learned Through Suffering

Many of us today are looking for spiritual experiences. We run here and there, from one revival to another, seeking spiritual gifts and anointing. But very early in her walk with the Lord, Jeanne Guyon realized that "spiritual experience" can get in the way. It can delay the work of the Holy Spirit in us, which is designed to bring us into what she called "true union" with Him. Writing about our need to seek nothing other than union with God, she says, "[The prayer that brings union with God]…is far above…transports or visions, for visions are in the inferior powers of the soul and cannot produce true union. The soul must not dwell or rely upon them or be impeded by them. They are but favors and gifts, the Giver alone must be our object and aim."[18]

In other words, she warns against overemphasis on visions, because they can be deceiving and can cause pride and vanity to arise. Instead of attending to and loving, extolling, and praising God, we can dwell on our gifts and visions, which can lead us astray.

Madame Guyon also warns against overemphasizing "spiritual feelings" or "ecstasies." She wrote, "Ecstasies arise from a perceptible delight. They may be termed a kind of spiritual sensuality, wherein the soul, by letting it go too far by reason of the sweetness it finds in them, falls imperceptibly into decay."[19]

She even goes on to warn us about "personal words" from God, which so many Christians seek today. "And as to distinct interior words," she warns, "they too are subject to illusion. The enemy can form and counterfeit them. But the immediate Word of God has neither tone nor articulation. It is mute, silent, and unutterable."[20]

Many of her most brilliant insights came to her in her

times of loss and desperate weakness. We have already seen how she learned to press into God as a young woman with everything against her. Later in life when she was ill and could no longer visit the poor she loved so dearly, she insisted that it was for love that God allowed even that which is most dear to your soul—your calling, gifting, or anointing—to fall away so that you might be drawn closer to Him alone.

Most importantly, Madame Guyon's life teaches us the wonderful truth about how we too can experience true intimacy with God. She wrote, "It is Jesus Christ Himself, the real and essential Word, who is in the center of the soul that is disposed for receiving Him. Never one moment ceases from His living fruitful, and divine operation."[21]

Her focus was on so loving the Lord and being so captivated by Him that she learned to bear all things with grace and humility. Because the character of Christ shone so strongly inside her, the enemy could never gain a foothold within.

May we who struggle to find God in our everyday lives learn the secret Madame Guyon knew so well. She said that "in all things, and everywhere, she found her proper center, because everywhere she found God."[22]

The hidden treasures Madame Guyon discovered were not found by her alone. She traveled a well-worn path tread upon by many others over the centuries. She was one of many women of the secret place whose lives were completely devoted and fully consecrated to knowing God.

Lord of my life, let me hear Your call. Separate me from the clamor of other voices and draw me to Yourself. I pray for the grace of having Your divine perspective, so that I can stay by Your side as I walk this journey of faith. Help me understand how You want to use my personal sufferings and grief for the sake of Your kingdom. Preserve me from distractions and worldly viewpoints. I want to grow closer to You every day. Always Yours, amen.

Chapter Four

Teresa of Avila *(1515–1582)*

POSSESSED BY GOD'S LOVE

On March 28, 1515, a light flickered in a dark chapter in Spanish history. A tiny girl was born in the small provincial Castilian town of Avila (City of Knights) in southern Spain. She was given the name Teresa de Cepeda y Ahumada.[1]

It was the height of the Spanish Inquisition, in a time in which thousands of Jews were being slaughtered under the reign of Queen Isabella and King Ferdinand. It was also a time of glaring contrasts, for in the midst of such darkness it was also a season of great adventure for Spain. During this century of gold, the Spanish Armada, the conquistadors, and Christopher Columbus were discovering vast stretches of the great unknown.

Teresa of Avila was born for such a time. She became a

beacon of light in an uncertain age, a messenger of the secret place of God's presence who modeled Christ as a place of safety, comfort, and certain refuge. Throughout her life, her soul would often be caught away to be with God, where she would be filled with visions of the Lover of her soul. She called Jesus "His Majesty." As she became well-known, her fellow countrymen called her "Teresa of Jesus" and a "Doctor of the Church." First and foremost, she simply loved God.

Childhood Years

Even as a young child, Teresa fiercely and passionately loved the Lord. She was the third child of her mother, the first daughter. Her father had three children by his first marriage and then nine by his second wife. So Teresa grew up in a large family and most of her siblings were boys.[2] Her father was Don Alonso Sanchez de Cepeda, the wealthy son of a Jewish merchant from Toledo.[3] Nevertheless, he read to his family every night about the great Christian martyrs.

Even as Teresa played childhood games with her little friends, her love for Jesus was never far from her mind. A favorite game was called "monks and nuns." At age seven, she convinced her brother Rodrigo to leave home with her in search of martyrdom at the hands of the Moors. (They were discovered just outside the city gates by their uncle and returned to their parents.)

Teresa was adventuresome, but while other children ran and played, Teresa sought for ways to be alone with her Lord. She prayed often and turned her bedroom at home into a sanctuary where she hung a picture of Christ speaking with the Samaritan woman at the well. Teresa pleaded over and over again in prayer, "Lord, give me of that water that I may not thirst."[4]

Her mother, Doria Beatriz de Ahumada, was not yet twenty years old when Teresa was born. Beatriz spent much of her life ill, lying in bed reading romance novels about a dark, handsome knight. Though her husband did not approve, Beatriz often read these romantic books to her children. By the time of Beatriz's death when Teresa was a young teen, it was clear these melodramas had greatly stimulated her lively imagination.

Consumed with vanity, Teresa flirted with young men and delighted in flattery, jewelry, parties, and clothing. All these things took the place of God in her life.

Life-Changing Experiences

One day, something shocking put an end to everything worldly in Teresa's life—she fell to the floor as if dead. Many believed that she lapsed into a coma, although little proof has been offered. Doctors found no pulse, and all attempts to revive her failed.

Thinking she was dead, the doctors left and a priest anointed her body with holy oil; prayers for the dead were recited and nuns set her body aside to stiffen before burial. The family made funeral preparations and a grave was prepared.

Four days later, her father and her brother witnessed a supernatural fire as it hit her body. Her eyelids began blinking, her arms moved, blood rushed to her face, and she rose from the bed inexplicably. While everyone had been thinking that Teresa was dead, she was having a heavenly vision, seeing her family and communities of nuns.

By the time Teresa turned sixteen, she had been involved in a relationship with a young man of whom her father did not approve. As a result, her father sent Teresa off to live in a strict Spanish convent school where her social life was drastically curtailed. When Teresa entered Avila's Convent of the Incarnation, she began to see that her previous assumptions about life were now behind her, and from that moment she wanted nothing to do with the world.

She was still unwell and in pain, and she convalesced at the convent for several years, continuing to slip in and out of consciousness at times. Sometimes, it appeared as if no life inhabited her body for weeks and she lay on her bed like a beautiful corpse. Yet, each time, Teresa would recover her senses.

Some time later, another dramatic event took place. Teresa had a spiritual encounter with God so intense that she eventually questioned her own sanity. She saw the risen Jesus, not through physical eyes but as in a vision through her heart. She was questioned by the nuns regarding her experience:

"How do you know it was Jesus?"

At the point of tears, she replied, "Because He told me so, over and over again."[5]

Though she had walked through a dark night of the soul with great physical pain and affliction, from this time on it seemed as though the tangible presence of Jesus was with her.

Another even more intense encounter awaited Teresa years later. In her autobiography, Teresa wrote of a shining angel plunging a flaming golden arrow into her heart. He thrust the fiery dart into her heart several times, leaving her with an intense love for God. She says, "When he drew it out I thought he was carrying off with him the deepest part of me; and he left me all on fire with a great love of God."[6] She described the angel as small and very beautiful. Reflecting upon this encounter, she considered that this angel from the Lord was so illuminated that he had to be one of the very highest of the angels—the cherubim.[7]

After Teresa's death, her heart was investigated, and it appeared to have been pierced through the center as if by a dart. As late as 1872, three physicians who were professors of surgery examined her heart. They reported that they found the heart still incorrupt (untouched by decomposition) almost three hundred years later. The heart was punctured on both sides, leaving a perforation through two of its chambers, verifying what Teresa called the "transverberation" of her heart.[8]

Teresa's superiors were skeptical of her visitations, some accusing her of being influenced by satanic powers. Nevertheless, Teresa soon gained a large following as stories of her many encounters spread. At times while meditating on the Lord, she would be raptured into His presence. She would go into ecstasy, seeing the Lord Jesus while receiving the Eucharist. Many writers say that Teresa of Avila had more documented trances and visions of heaven and the Lord Jesus than any other person in all of church history. She was a "Christian mystic" in the truest sense.

Teresa's Life of Prayer

In her early forties, Teresa's inner life acquired an entirely fresh dimension. She spoke about her life in God in an analogy, describing it as "a new book—I mean of a new life in prayer which God has given to me."[9] She also described her life of prayer as a garden already planted, but one in which the plants will die unless they are tended and watered carefully. She said that such nurturing can be accomplished four ways: (1) the laborious work of carefully drawing water from the well, (2) the slightly easier method of using a waterwheel and buckets, (3) by means of a stream running through the garden, saturating the ground from beneath, and (4) the best method of all, the rain, the natural source of water, which entails no work at all on the part of the gardener but which comes from heaven above.[10]

Teresa used these descriptive terms to paint a vivid picture of the stages of cultivating a life of prayer. The beginner toils, fetching water from the well. The effort is entirely his, as he attempts to fill his bucket with water with which to revive the flowers of the garden. If he persists, his love for the flowers will exceed the strain of work. The privilege of seeing the arid land blossom will produce humility and endurance that will cause his soul to prosper richly.

In the second stage of prayer, the gardener uses a waterwheel and buckets. He can draw more water for the garden than before with much less effort, but long hours are still required. This kind of prayer can be a time of trial, with weeding and pruning being done within the soul. Here the believer learns the Prayer of Quiet and the beginning of pure contemplation. Effort is still necessary, but the place of striving eases and receptivity is better understood.

The third stage of prayer is when the Lord is more active, providing water by a spring or stream running through the garden. There is now no question of turning back, the delight is too sweet; it is a "glorious folly, a heavenly madness in which true wisdom is acquired."[11] Teresa said this was when Mary and Martha, contemplation and action, are in perfect harmony, though not yet entirely absorbed into God. The soul is free from worries and becomes content. God is now the gardener and the supply of water is abundant.

The last stage of the call to the secret place is where the garden is watered by rain and the gardener has nothing to do but to watch the flowers grow. This is what Madame Jeanne Guyon and many others called the Prayer of Union. The rain brings this union about from heaven itself. After this type of prayer, Teresa found herself in a state of overwhelming tenderness, bathed in tears of joy. At this stage, you know God and you experience great and sweet delight.

Love was what it was all about to Teresa; her life of prayer was the story of an intimate friendship with God. Teresa of Avila and others who have known the secret place have cherished the inner courts of the Lord. They followed in the paths of other forerunners who had gone before them, and their authentic inward journey led to empowered outward works.

Her Call to Reform and Renewal

While at Avila's Convent of the Incarnation, Teresa began noticing worldly habits among the nuns there—gossip, slander, and vanity. Many of the women were more concerned about physical matters than spiritual ones. The sisters occasionally indulged in irreverence and disorder, which the house's lax rules allowed. Teresa felt that few of them understood her visions or wanted to achieve a high level of intimacy with God. These concerns formed the basis for her lifelong effort to reform the Carmelite Order. With little support from her peers and no guidance from others, Teresa began searching for a way to be of greater practical use to God. And out of her hidden life in God she found what she needed to cause vital changes.

When Teresa requested that the Catholic Church permit her to live in poverty and serve the poor, a fierce controversy arose. At the time, women were considered so "radically inferior" to men, that the thought of a lone woman roaming the countryside having spiritual encounters roused the objections of more than a few religious authorities. In fact, Teresa herself held reservations about women, and was once quoted as saying, "I would not want you to be womanish in anything, nor would I want you to be like women, but like strong men. For if you do what is in your power, the Lord will make you so strong that you will astonish men." Teresa continued, "I am not at all like women…for I have a robust spirit."[12]

In her book *Teresa of Avila,* Carmelite nun Tessa Bielecki suggests that such statements from Teresa served two purposes: (1) to present her opinion on feminine weakness, and (2) to downplay her own femininity so as to avoid attention from the Inquisition and its scrutiny of women in the church.[13]

In 1562, when Teresa reached the age of forty-seven, she founded a new convent. There she spent many years teaching young women about God and her "reformed way of life."[14] She wrote two works, *The Way of Perfection* and *Meditations on the Song of Songs.* Later in April 1567, the Father General of the Carmelite Order gave Teresa permission to found more new convents abroad. In August of the same year, she took to the road and met a man called John of the Cross while founding Medina del Campo. Teresa eventually cofounded three convents together with John of the Cross, whom she considered her spiritual advisor. Teresa planted convents at Pastrana and Toledo in 1569, Salamanca in 1570, Alba de Tormes in 1571, and in several other locations over the years.

After Teresa established Alba of Tormes, religious authorities suddenly pulled her away from her tasks abroad and placed Teresa back at the Convent of the Incarnation, the place where she began her life as a nun. Despite her objections, she received the title of "prioress" for one term in the convent. Though she had spent many years there previously, Teresa noticed a severe lack of enthusiasm for her return. She was disliked and unwelcome. To combat the division and rebellion, she invited her good friend John of the Cross to take the position of chaplain, figuring that spiritual guides and friends are needed by all.

Friends and Guides to Teresa

Thanks to the combined efforts of Teresa and John of the Cross, the convent soon returned to order and harmony.

Teresa felt God Himself had helped them through John, in effect disguising Himself as a man as He also had done with Moses' burning bush. John of the Cross became the first Carmelite friar, a mystical poet, and a Doctor of the Church.

When Teresa's term as prioress was completed, together she and John of the Cross launched out again and founded another convent, this time at Segovia. Two were better than one, and over the years their teamwork yielded excellent results.

In April 1575, Teresa met the man who would become her closest friend and advisor, Jeronimo Gracian. She called Gracian "my helper" and prayed that he would assist her in the Carmelite reform. Teresa once wrote, "I have been suffering from these Fathers of the Cloth for more than seventeen years with not a soul to help me, and it was too much for my poor strength—I did not know how to bear it any longer."[15]

Later that year, persecution as a result of her reform efforts escalated to new heights. A vengeful princess who had twice been expelled from one of Teresa's convents for outrageous behavior denounced her to the Inquisition. Betrayal followed denunciation as the Father General of the Carmelites, a man named Rubeo, originally a great encourager of Teresa's work, switched sides and began to disapprove publicly of her ministry. All Teresa's relationships, especially those with men, came under fire. Ambiguous rumors about sexuality slandered her chaste love for Gracian, and villains working for the Inquisition kidnapped John of the Cross and imprisoned him for nine months. The leaders of the

Inquisition eventually ordered Teresa to relocate to a convent of her choosing in Castile. She lost much approval and popularity, as her life's work, her message, and the reformation efforts became vulnerable. Nevertheless, her spirit continued to burn for God.

The Interior Castle

In 1577, between June 2 and November 29, Teresa wrote her most famous work on prayer, called *The Interior Castle,* known in Spanish as *Las Moradas* (The Mansions). This now-classic book is the most profound of her mystical works; it is based on the analogy of the journey and transformation of a silkworm into a beautiful butterfly. *Las Moradas* outlines a perfect balance between the inner and the outer works of the Holy Spirit in the believer's life.

The Interior Castle was written following an extremely vivid vision, which portrayed the soul of man as on a progressive journey through a castle with many rooms. John 14:2a tells us that, "My father's house has many rooms." So it is in the life of each disciple. We are temples of the living God, and He has taken up royal residence within us. In allegorical language, Teresa wrote about seven rooms that an ardent believer passes through on the journey to perfect union with God. She said, "The figure is used to describe the whole course of the mystical life—the soul's progress from the first mansion to the seventh and its transformation from an imperfect and sinful creature into the Bride of the Spiritual Marriage."[16]

The first mansion or room typifies the earliest and most basic stages of the Christian walk. Those at this stage know God but still retain much of the world's influence. Numerous temptations pull at the soul, which is unable to appreciate the beauty of the castle or to find any peace with it. To progress onto the second room, one must begin to learn the lessons of humility.

To enter the second mansion requires a person to understand the need to respond to God's call, desiring to leave the world behind and gradually coming nearer to the place where His Majesty (God) dwells. His beckoning call can be heard more often, more endearingly, more convictingly, and more clearly than ever before. The seeker must begin to understand that the One whose voice is calling from the deep is supposed to be his or her best friend forever, from that time forward.

In the third mansion of the Interior Castle, the seeker has developed a measure of discipline and virtue in life. But when reason steps in to replace love and virtuous living and God's grace, lessons of mercy are in order. Nothing can be received from Him without His great love, grace, and mercy.

The fourth room is captivating, for it is here that the mystical dimension or Spirit of revelation is released. The voice of the soul becomes diminished, and the waters of life rise higher. Here the seeker enters deeper into the Prayer of Quiet and finds consolation from God Himself. This sense of intimacy with the beloved Bridegroom entices the Bride to proceed forward into the fifth room, where the metaphor of the silkworm is introduced. Here the imagery of metamorphosis and the power of transformation help us to embrace the lessons of death to self and life unto God. Seekers now become spiritual lovers, and betrothal is now the goal.

The sixth mansion is one of growing intimacy with the Lover of one's soul, in addition to increasing levels of tribulation, trials, and times of testing. But also in this chamber a flood of heavenly favors from God is bestowed upon His Beloved, which intensifies the holy desire for oneness with the Lord. The one who has pursued God so passionately becomes clothed in the garments of His presence.

The seventh and final room in Teresa's extraordinary Interior Castle is that of Spiritual Marriage itself, where complete transformation, perfect peace, and dwelling in the King's wonderful presence are realized. Here Teresa wrote, "That union is like two wax candles that are joined so that the light now given off is but one. Or it is as if a tiny streamlet enters the sea from which it will find no way of separating itself (nor want to) from the sea of God's immense great love."[17]

No one who makes the inward journey to the place of intimate communion with the Lord will ever be the same again. That innermost chamber of our hearts where one meets Him face-to-face is not only a sanctuary of sweet fellowship, a blissful fulfillment of holy desire, but also a place of glorious transformation. Like St. Teresa's silkworm, those who enter that realm as humble, earthbound souls, emerge as beautiful butterflies, with their souls ready to take wing and soar.

Teresa's Legacy

We each leave a shadow in this life that will fall upon others. That is what happens when people walk in the light of God's love; the shadow of His presence is cast upon others from our lives. Teresa's legacy was that the secret place became her dwelling place, despite poor health that only became increasingly fragile as she grew older. (Her eventual death surprised very few people.)

An acting Provincial called Antonio of Jesus sent her on an unexpected journey to Alba de Tormes. He was jealous, cold, and insensitive to Teresa's ill health and physical needs. She humbly obeyed his orders, contrary to the advice of friends. Hunger and terrible pain marked her journey. On October 4, 1582, after finally reaching Alba de Tormes, the ailing Teresa of Jesus died from exhaustion and near starvation. With a heart of obedience, humility, and the completed work of His Majesty, she was ushered into sweet comfort and eternal heavenly bliss.

Perhaps the best way to sum up the life of Teresa is in her own words written toward the end of her life. Listen to her through them, for they describe this mystical poet's great trust.

> Let nothing trouble you,
> Let nothing scare you,
> All is fleeing,

God alone is unchanging,
Patience,
Everything obtains.
Who possesses God nothing wants.
God alone suffices.[18]

Chapter Five

✝

Fanny Crosby *(1820-1915)*

SONGS FROM THE SECRET PLACE

Fanny Crosby was the queen of gospel music during the late nineteenth and early twentieth century, capturing a vision of God's secret place in thousands of hymns, which continue to be sung by God's people today. Her hymns still ignite spiritual passion from east and west, and when they were first published, hymns such as "Pass Me Not, O Gentle Savior" and "Saved By Grace" were sung by believers in Arab nations, Germany, and even by Queen Victoria of England and the Prince and Princess of Wales.

Noted hymn writer and evangelical singer George Stebbins said of Fanny, "There is no character in the history of the American Sunday school and evangelistic hymns so outstanding as that of Fanny Crosby, and it is quite as true that more of her hymns than of any other writer of the nineteenth century have found an abiding place in the hearts of Christians the world over. So evident is this that there is a fragrance about her very name that no other has.

"There was probably no other writer in her day who appealed more to the valid experience of the Christian life or who expressed more sympathetically the deep longings of the human heart than Fanny Crosby."[1]

In her prime, Fanny Crosby was considered of equal stature with colleagues D. L. Moody and Ira Sankey. She was renowned as a preacher and lecturer, and spent much of her life involved in home missions. People would line up for blocks to hear her speak.

She didn't start writing until she was in her forties; nevertheless, she wrote about nine thousand hymns. Her style was revolutionary for her day. Instead of mimicking the traditional, old-fashioned hymn language, she expressed thoughts and prayers in common words that touched the heart of worship in believers. Her obvious passion for God drew the lost into His kingdom.

Fanny also composed more than a thousand poems, and she played the harp and organ in concert. So many accomplishments seem incredible for any one person, but all the more when you realize that this woman was blind from infancy.

A Flowing River of Spiritual Expression

How was such fiery passion kindled in Fanny Crosby? How did she discover this river of spiritual expression and experience it in person? Let's journey together through the milestones of Fanny Crosby's life in search of some of the keys God used to unlock the secret place within her heart.

Fanny was born into a rural family that was fiercely proud of its history and heritage. Their lineage could be traced back to William Brewster, who sailed on the Mayflower in 1620 and was a founding father of Plymouth Plantation. Fanny's grandfather, Sylvanus, a hardworking farmer, fought in the War of 1812. Mercy, his oldest daughter, married a man named John Crosby, who was nearly as old as Sylvanus and probably a distant cousin. John and Mercy lived with her parents to help on the farm. Mercy was twenty years old when she delivered Frances Jane (Fanny) Crosby into the world on March 24, 1820.

Fanny's childhood home was in Gayville, located in the town of Southeast, in rural Putnam County, New York. There, eleven families made up the Crosby clan, and all who lived in the Southeast community wore Puritan-style clothing. Women's dresses were black with full skirts and white collars and cuffs. The community held strict Calvinistic beliefs, which included the sovereignty of God's grace, divine predestination, eternal security of the believer, total depravity of mankind, and the supreme authority of the Word of God. Children learned long passages of Scripture, received just enough education to read and write, and did farm work alongside their parents.

Damaged Vision

Fanny was about a month old when her parents noticed something was wrong with her eyes. Medical help was difficult to find in their little community, so when the family found a man who claimed to be a physician, they entrusted Fanny to his care. He placed hot poultices on the baby's inflamed eyes and told the parents the poultices would draw the infection out. The infection did leave, but Fanny's eyes were left with ugly white scars, and her vision was damaged. As a result she had little more than some light perception.

A second tragedy happened to the Crosby family that same year. In November 1820, Fanny's father, John, died from exposure after working in the fields in cold, rainy weather. To supplement the family's income, twenty-one-year-old Mercy had to take work as a maidservant for a wealthy family nearby. Mercy's grandmother Eunice cared for Fanny.

Grandmother Eunice took a great interest in her granddaughter, and the two became very close during the first five years of Fanny's life. With the passage of time, it became painfully apparent Fanny would not regain her sight, and Eunice was determined to give Fanny every advantage in training she could think of. She could not bear to see Fanny going through life being treated as a helpless invalid, utterly dependent on others.

Fanny's education began as she sat with her family in the evenings listening as a family member read by the fireplace such works as *The Iliad, The Odyssey, Paradise Lost, The Tales of Robin Hood,* and the Bible. Eunice became her granddaughter's eyes, describing her surroundings to her in careful detail. Because Fanny could at times distinguish certain hues, Eunice was able to help bring definition to colors.

She taught Fanny in a very holistic manner. If she used the word "bristle," for example, she would place in Fanny's hands an object with bristles, to correspond to the meaning of the word. When she taught Fanny about birds, she would include the song of a particular bird, its size, shape, coloring, and the shape of its wings. She taught Fanny botany and every subject she knew. Grandmother and granddaughter would take walks together, and Eunice would describe the different types of trees and flowers. Fanny was taught by smell and touch; the leaves she knew by "handling and remembering."[2]

After thoroughly teaching her granddaughter, Eunice would test her. She would gather a pile of leaves, and one by one place them in Fanny's hands. Then she would ask, "Now, what tree is this one from?"[3] Fanny absorbed everything and developed an incredible memory and an amazing talent to communicate through description.

Her grandmother taught her about God as well. Eunice had the rare gift of seeing God in all of creation; to her, creation was a mirror that reflected spiritual truth. In all their walks together in the woods and through the fields, Eunice illuminated the idea that she and Fanny were not alone, but God was walking with them. She taught Fanny that every bird, tree, and flower had been designed by God to serve His plans and purposes. Eunice taught Fanny about the loving nature of a wonderful God.

Fanny's mother, Mercy, continued laboring outside the home to earn money to support Fanny. Unfortunately, she would return home at night too tired to spend much time with her much-beloved daughter. When Mercy became weighed down with weariness and worry about her daughter's future, Eunice would offer strength and support. She would come close, place her hand on Mercy's shoulder, and recite a part of a favorite hymn, or she'd quote a favorite old adage of Puritan leader Cotton Mather: "What can't be cured can be endured."

Grandmother Eunice Plants Seeds of Faith

Grandmother Eunice loved gathering children together to read the Bible, explaining its stories in language that they could understand. "The stories of the Holy Book came from her lips and entered my heart and took deep root there," said Fanny later.[4] Eunice often reminded the children about "a kind heavenly Father who sent His only son, Jesus Christ, into this world to be the Savior and friend of all mankind."[5]

Eunice was a "firm believer in prayer," and understood it was the key to a successful Christian life. She considered prayer a "close communication with her loving Savior."[6] Everything she believed about God and the importance and place of prayer was freely poured into Fanny. Grandmother taught little Fanny how to call on God for every need, and how to trust in His goodness, certain authority, and power to accomplish every good work and to care for every need.

This is how Fanny learned to trust Jesus Christ, how to rest and rejoice in Him. This wise grandmother's classroom imparted to Fanny a deep faith and an ability to bear her sufferings and difficulties with great grace and joy, knowing that God was always walking with her, leading and guiding and loving her.

The little Southeast community church lacked an organ, and the congregation did not sing hymns that would be familiar in most of today's church services. Like the early Puritans, they did not believe in hymns of human composition. They used the "music" of the Psalms, which they felt had been dictated from God to David, and they chanted them without any musical accompaniment. The only person in the church with a copy of the hymn was a deacon who stood at the podium or desk. He would recite a line of the psalm and then the congregation would repeat it after him until they had recited the entire psalm.

This form of worship created a hunger in Fanny's heart for greater expression. To her it was lifeless. Fanny loved singing and fed her soul listening to the music of nature. She wanted to experience all that life had to offer and did not consider herself to be different from other children, except when someone would make a comment to that effect. She was a happy and contented child. Eunice and Mercy would let Fanny play outside at night with the other children of the town within the vicinity of their house. For blind Fanny, playing at night was not anything unusual.

When Fanny was five years old, Mercy took her to the Columbia University School of Medicine, in New York City, to be examined by Dr. Valentine Mott, considered one of the top surgeons in the United States. He confirmed Mercy's worst fears, that the "doctor" who had treated Fanny's eyes had done irreparable damage. Mercy comforted her daughter by assuring her that God had a special plan and purpose for her life. On the way home, Fanny had an experience with God.

"As I sat there on the deck amid the glories of the departing day, the low murmur of the waves soothed my soul into a delightful peace. Their music was translated into tones that were like a human voice...."[7] The experience touched Fanny deeply.

Mercy landed a new housekeeping job that required mother and daughter to move six miles away from their present home. Everything changed for Fanny, because her mother was much more apt to apply the rod freely for correction, in contrast to Grandmother's gentler approach. Nevertheless, Mercy truly loved her daughter and cared for her needs as well as she could. Fanny learned to climb trees "like a squirrel," rode horseback, and climbed stone walls.

Eunice visited often and continued teaching Fanny many things. As a blind person, Fanny seemed to be able to do almost anything a sighted person could. Still, she went through times of discouragement. She would ask God "whether, in all His great world, he had not some little place for me."

In response, Fanny heard Him reply, "Do not be discouraged, little girl. You shall someday be happy and useful, even in your blindness."[8]

Fanny's First Poem

Fanny composed her first work when she was eight years old; it reads as follows:

Oh, what a happy child I am,
Although I cannot see!
I am resolved that in this world
Contented I will be!
How many blessings I enjoy
That other people don't!
So weep or sigh because I'm blind,
I cannot—nor I won't.

A year later, Mercy acquired another new position, and she moved with Fanny to Ridgefield, Connecticut, where the little girl was destined to receive another installment in her training. Mrs. Hawley, the landlady who cared for Fanny while Mercy was at work, made it a goal for Fanny to memorize the entire Bible.

Fanny learned a few chapters each week. She mastered Genesis, Exodus, Leviticus, Numbers, and the four Gospels by the end of the year. Within two years, she had also memorized many of the Psalms, all of Proverbs, Ruth, and the Song of Solomon. She carried on this task throughout the rest of her life. Gradually, she eliminated the need for someone to read the Bible to her; she had absorbed every word of it into her mind and heart.

Mrs. Hawley also included selections from secular works for Fanny to memorize, including various poems of the day. Fanny was introduced to the hymns of Charles Wesley and Isaac Watts when she would occasionally visit a Methodist church, and she loved their majestic sound.

As Fanny reached adolescence, she became increasingly

troubled about her handicap. She began competing with her friends, trying to prove what a blind person could do. She also spent many hours thinking, poring over the Scriptures. She felt more and more alone. Finally one night, she was able to talk to her grandmother about this ache in her heart. They prayed together, and Fanny remembered the night. It "was beautiful. I crept toward the window, and through the branches of a giant oak that stood just outside, the soft moonlight fell upon my head like the benediction of an angel, while I knelt there and repeated over and over these simple words: 'Dear Lord, please show me how I can learn like other children.'"[9] She felt an immediate release from the anxiety that had weighed her down. It was "changed to the sweet consciousness that my prayer would be answered in due time."[10]

"By the Grace of God, I Will"

On a summer evening in 1831, Fanny and her grandmother would be together one last time. Eunice had become very ill and knew she was about to die. She told Fanny, "Grandma's going home." In her soft, frail voice she asked, "Tell me, my darling, will you meet Grandma in our Father's house on high?"

Fanny responded, "By the grace of God, I will." Eunice drew Fanny to herself one last time, and they prayed their last prayer together. Eunice Crosby died a short time later, at the age of 53.[11]

Those early years laid the foundation stones of preparation in Fanny's life. She discovered a wonderful singing talent, learned to play the guitar, became an accomplished horsewoman, and developed a reputation as a storyteller. But where she really shone was in her poetry, which enabled her to burst into fulfillment of God's purpose for her life.

At age fourteen, a wonderful door of opportunity opened. Fanny enrolled in the New York Institution for the Blind, where she would spend the next twenty years of her life. There she was educated in English grammar, science, music, history, philosophy, astronomy, and political economy; and she learned Braille, although she struggled with it. (Her fingertips had become callused from playing guitar, which made it difficult to feel the raised letters.) She memorized the complete text of Brown's Grammar.

Fanny's enthusiasm for poetry continued to grow, but her teachers at the Institution felt she was letting this ability "puff up her head." One of her instructors reprimanded her, telling her "not to think too much about rhymes and the praises that come from them." At first she was hurt, but then, "through tears, she composed herself, threw her arms around his neck, and kissed his forehead. 'You have talked to me as my father would have if he were living. And I thank you for it.'"[12]

She continued to grow in her education and various talents and skills, and at the age of twenty was considered the institution's most promising student. She showed such promise in her poetic talent that she was given a poetic composition teacher named Hamilton Murray. Mr. Murray played an invaluable role in her training. He gave her long poems to memorize and taught her the use of rhyme, rhythm, and meter, as well as encouraged her to imitate well-known poets.

Fanny absorbed the rudiments and refinements of poetry, and learned to compose quickly. This thorough training was the foundation stone that would later enable her to compose as many as twelve poems a day. She became known as "the blind poetess."

Visitors to the institute would be shown the works of its brightest students. US President John Tyler, New York Governor William Henry Seward, and Count Bertrand, Napoleon's field marshal, were just a few who visited. During her time with the school, first as student, then later as instructor, Fanny contributed to various New York poetry columns and published four books of poetry. She knew her recognition as "the blind poetess" was gaining much-needed attention for the institute and for the needs of the blind, and she was delighted to serve in this way, harboring no particular aspirations of attaining a greater personal platform.

Called to the Secret Place

In 1848, cholera broke out and Fanny contracted the disease. She recovered, but her close brush with death made her think about dying. Would she be ready to meet God? She had believed in God and His goodness but had never experienced conversion. During this time of seeking and soul-searching, Fanny dreamed she visited a dying man. The man asked her if she would meet him in heaven after their deaths. She responded in the dream that by God's help, she would—the same response she had given her grandmother.

The dream ended as the man said, "Remember, you promised a dying man!"

The experience drew Fanny to a deeper place of seeking God. She attended revival meetings and went to the altar twice, feeling nothing had changed. However, the third time she went to the altar, something happened.

Bonnie C. Harvey, author of the book *Fanny Crosby: Woman of Faith,* describes what occurred: "During the fifth verse of 'Alas and Did My Savior Bleed?' Fanny prayed, 'Here Lord, I give myself away. 'Tis all that I can do.' Suddenly Fanny felt 'my very soul was flooded with celestial light.' She jumped to her feet, shouting, 'Hallelujah! Hallelujah!' She said, 'For the first time I realized that I had been trying to hold the world in one hand and the Lord in the other.'"[13]

Fanny's life was dramatically changed. She called it her "November experience." From that point on, her life was totally dedicated to God. A desire to do His will alone consumed her, and all other desires fell away. It was out of this experience that many of her later hymns were born. One unpublished poem, called "Valley of Silence," explains more than any other of Fanny's writings her mystical experience of November 20, 1850. She wrote this poem two months before she died:

> I walk down the Valley of Silence,
> Down the dim, voiceless valley alone,
> And I hear not the fall of a footstep
> Around me, save God's and my own;
> And the hush of my heart is as holy

As hours when angels have flown.
Long ago I was weary of voices
Whose music my heart could not win,
Long ago I was weary of noises
That fretted my soul with their din;
Long ago I was weary with places,
When I met but the human and sin.
Do you ask what I found in this Valley?
'Tis my trysting place with the Divine,
For I fell at the feet of the Holy,
And above me a voice said, "Be Mine."
And there rose from the depth of my spirit,
The echo, "My heart shall be Thine."
Do you ask how I live in this Valley?
I weep and I dream and I pray;
But my tears are so sweet as the dewdrops
That fall from the roses in May,
And my prayer, like a perfume from censers,
Ascendeth to God night and day.

The sweetness and nearness of God is so evident in this poem. Fanny surely knew the call to the secret place. She moved forward with her life, married, and had a child (who, sadly, died in infancy). She met presidents and befriended influential people. God blessed Fanny by linking her with songwriters who could open doors to share her hymns with the masses of Christians who needed to have their faith bolstered.

Living during the time when the national Sunday school

movement was sweeping the nation, when mission societies were proliferating, and when a revival called the Second Great Awakening was shaking America, Fanny found plenty of opportunities to put her well-honed talent to work. Her years of preparation through hardship and poverty had refined her heart into gold that was now ready to be poured out into the world.

Gold Poured Out to the World

How did she find the secret place in God? From which treasures of her life experiences can we glean and learn? Let's now examine some of these treasures, take them into our own hearts, and deeply cherish them.

For a child to have a mentor is truly God's gift, and Fanny had a wonderful mentor in her grandmother Eunice. Eunice taught her to believe in the goodness and faithfulness of God. Believing is the antidote to bitterness, resentment, and fear. Fanny literally was led by the hand and walked through pastures, woods, and valleys as she was taught of God's faithfulness in creation. Grandmother Eunice taught young Fanny to look for and find God in every place and every situation. He is always there, but we have to be taught to expect to find Him.

The Bible tells us to renew our minds by meditating on the Scripture. Fanny certainly did. In order to find God's secret place, we must discover markers to point the way, and reading and meditating on God's Word permits our Father to speak to us about what's important to Him. He longs to share His secrets. The power, illumination, and transformation that come to us through God's Word are beyond description.

Fanny associated with the poor in spirit, slum dwellers, alcoholics, and prisoners. She gave herself to a life of simplicity, giving away money and aid to those in need. She knew God's heart for the poor and needy, and in embracing them she embraced Him. One of the keys to the secret place is cultivating a tender heart for the alien, the orphan, and the widow.

Fanny did not equate giftedness with godliness, and she was never "holier than thou." She freely gave away the gift that God deposited within her. She wrote under at least 204 pen names, and she wrote verses for friends who published them with their own melodies. No one actually knows just how many hymns and poems she wrote. It did not matter to her who got the credit, as long as God could be glorified.

Fanny understood the power of distraction and would purposely take time alone with God in the long night watches. Every day, she found a place to be alone with Him, even when it meant sleepless nights. He was her rest and peace.

Fanny learned how to apply herself, employing all her energies to realize the full maturity and effectiveness of her gifting. She harnessed the strength of her mind to the Spirit of God, thus enabling her mind to become an effective tool. She brought her mental ability into the secret place with her.

By learning to embrace criticism from others, Fanny remained humble all her life. She established a lifestyle of selflessness, not giving room in her heart to pride. She learned to receive from God and others, whether in gentleness or in conflict, and she knew how to ask God to make her heart right within her.

The grace of God is boundless, and His Truth is unending. We are on a journey in which we never "arrive" until the day we enter heaven's gates. Fanny Crosby is there now, beholding His face. God's gift through her is still giving life and hope to countless people, continuing to light the way to that secret place in God. In Fanny's own words:

> Savior, more than life to me,
> I am clinging, clinging close to Thee;
> Let Thy precious blood applied
> Keep me ever near Thy side.
> Every day, every hour,
> Let me feel Thy cleansing power;
> May Thy tender love to me
> Bind me closer, closer, Lord to Thee.

Chapter Six

━━━

Susanna Wesley *(1669–1742)*

THE MOTHER
OF REVIVAL

When more than two thousand Puritan pastors were threatened to stop practicing their faith by English Royalist officials under King Charles II, Dr. Samuel Annesley flatly refused. The consequences of opposing the king of England were harsh. Samuel was evicted from his clerical position and harassed. Still, he never wavered from his courageous convictions. Born into this tumultuous time was Samuel's impressionable youngest daughter, Susanna.

England had become embattled in a religious civil war. Royalists had fought for King Charles I and the Church of England against the Parliamentarians who sided with the Puritans, a religious sect that had separated from the Church of England. The Parliamentarians emerged as the initial victors, but a few years later, the Royalist army with King

Charles II regained power. Consequently, in 1662 legislation was passed forcing all ministers to conform to the practices and beliefs of the Church of England. This legislation was called the Act of Uniformity. When two thousand Puritan pastors refused to conform, the Great Ejection followed.

After ten years, King Charles II recanted somewhat and decided to permit a certain amount of religious freedom. Samuel then started a new ministry, reaching out to the poor, the fatherless, and the widows in London. Growing up in the midst of these events, Susanna's heart was imprinted with the basic principles of Christianity.

A Mother of Superior Understanding

Susanna Annesley was born in London on January 20, 1669, the twenty-fifth child of Dr. and Mrs. Annesley. (Of that number, records show only seven surviving to maturity.) The Annesleys were deeply devout Puritans, wholeheartedly committed to raising their children to fear the Lord. Susanna's mother was deeply loved and honored by her husband. She appears to have been a woman of superior understanding and earnest, consistent piety, devoted to promoting the religious welfare of all her children.

Samuel found great fulfillment in educating people in the ways of the Lord. He could not remember a time when he did not know Him. At five years of age, he began reading twenty chapters of the Bible every day. After graduating from Oxford University in 1644, he had become the pastor of a church in the county of Kent, where the people expressed their gratitude for his ministry. Later, he moved the family to London.

Susanna grew into a very accomplished young lady. She pursued the study of many subjects, including other religious beliefs and the political views of the day. Her parents provided her with a thorough knowledge of the Bible and a well-rounded education, although it was uncommon for girls to be formally educated in those days. Susanna excelled. She studied logic, metaphysics, philosophy, and theology. She also became proficient in French and in English grammar. Digging deeply into the religious controversy that had engulfed England, Susanna entered into debates alongside her father and his guests as they discussed these difficult matters. Before she was thirteen years old, Susanna already had studied the entire controversy between the Church of England and the Dissenters, and she had gained the respect of her elders for her opinions and insights.

As it turned out, having been raised in a family that was considered to be radical in its beliefs and uncompromising in its principles gave Susanna a solid foundation that would serve her well in the years to come.

Susanna met her future husband, whose name was also Samuel, in her parent's home. He was often a guest of her father and participated in the discussions in which Susanna took part. Samuel Wesley also came from a long family line of nonconformists, and his father was a minister who had been affected by the Great Ejection of 1662.

Samuel Wesley's father had held meetings in secret and had been imprisoned four times. He had died at the age of forty-two, when Samuel was quite young, and his son had been sent to various academies in London. During these years, he became convinced that he should join the established Church of England, so he had turned away from his Puritan roots.

At the time he made this decision, he and Susanna were probably discussing these matters together. Separately but simultaneously, they both made the same decision to join the Church of England, and in late 1688 or early 1689, they were married.

Love and Commitment

Samuel and Susanna had very different temperaments. Samuel was outgoing and jovial. Unfortunately, he was also a poor money manager, which created great difficulty for the couple throughout their life together. Susanna was introverted and quiet; she gave little attention to humor. She was very methodical in her approach to life, and though she was very passionate, she kept her emotions in check. Despite their strong personalities and great differences, Susanna and Samuel loved each other very much. Samuel lavished praise and respect upon Susanna. In the years of their marriage, their love and commitment for each other was greatly tested.

Two years after their marriage, in 1690, their first son, Samuel, was born. Then came Susanna in 1691. Emilia followed in 1692. Susanna's body became afflicted with rheumatism and other ailments because of the physical strain of her pregnancies being so close together. In 1694, little Susanna died, which must have been terribly painful for Susanna and Samuel. Twin boys were born at the end of

1694, named Annesley and Jedediah, but both died after only one month. In 1695, Sukey was born. Her given name was Susanna, after her deceased sister. Child number seven came along in 1696, named Mary, and then Hetty came in 1697.

At this time, the growing family received a new ministerial assignment. It promised to bring an increase in salary, and the rectory was supposed to be larger and more suitable for their large family. Actually, it turned out to be a hardship. The house and outbuildings were in great need of repair, Samuel's debts multiplied, and children were being added to their family at the rate of at least one per year. This period of time brought them to the brink of marital crisis.

A second set of twins was born in 1701, a boy and a girl. The infants must have died shortly after their birth, because they never were named. After baby Anne was born late in 1702, their financial difficulty increased even more, causing a marital crisis that climaxed with Samuel leaving Susanna and the children for a period of time. As Samuel was on his way to London, he learned that their house had caught fire. He returned home immediately, and the realization that he nearly lost his entire family brought him to his senses. He remained at home, repaired the house, and resumed his clerical duties. He and Susanna made a fresh start, forgiving each other and putting the whole difficult time behind them.

John Wesley came along in 1703, followed by his brother Charles in 1705. Both John and Charles entered the world in a very fragile state, but as time passed their health improved.

The Wesley family endured many hateful acts at the

hands of the people from the surrounding area. Much of the general population did not want to have anything to do with God or the Church, and many people vented their feelings by rampaging with impunity. The Wesleys were threatened, their fields were set ablaze, their cattle were attacked, and the children were often put to bed at night to the sound of gunfire in the streets. The children were afraid and rarely went outside. Another one of the children died.

Adding to the family's difficulty, a creditor had Samuel imprisoned for a debt of thirty pounds, which forced Susanna and the children to live on the earnings from their tiny dairy and the scant amount of money she had. Through these terribly sorrowful and difficult times, Samuel was impressed by his wife's resilient and steadfast spirit.

God Spared Their Son

A terrible fire occurred in the dead of winter in February 1709, probably set by mean-spirited local townspeople. Not only did it ravage their possessions, but it also almost took little John Wesley's life. He was saved by a neighbor who rescued him from the second story. Susanna lost all her books, her teaching papers, and her family treasures. Nevertheless, she was grateful to God for sparing her son's life.

After the fire, Samuel and Susanna, along with two-year-old Charles, went to live with one of their few friends. Their nineteenth and final child, Kezia, was born at this time. The rest of the children were sent to live in various homes until Susanna and Samuel could reestablish their household. Susanna learned the difficult lesson of trusting God completely in the face of disaster and years of real physical and emotional need. She did not surrender to despair but found strength in her sense of abandonment to God's care. Knowing that she was the Lord's, she believed that He could do with her life as He pleased.

Samuel completed repairs on their home, this time with fire-resistant bricks, and the Wesley family was reunited. Still, the neighboring people clung to their harsh judgments against them and continued to wish them harm.

Although 1712 began in hardship, Samuel Wesley felt it necessary to attend a religious convocation in London. Besides bringing even more financial stress upon the family with his travel and lodging expenses and having to pay a curate to care for his parish, it also meant he would be absent from his family for months on end.

While he was away, five of the children came down with smallpox. In addition, the temporary curate began working to undermine Samuel's position, purposely preaching about the evils of indebtedness, knowing full well that it was an unresolved issue in Samuel Wesley's life. Susanna was in a difficult place. The church lacked genuine spiritual guidance, her husband was being openly disrespected, and she disagreed with this man's policy of having only one church service on Sunday.

With her children's welfare in mind, Susanna decided to hold meetings in their kitchen on Sunday evenings. She included not only her children but the servants also. They sang psalms and read prayers. She preached a sermon taken from Samuel's library. Word spread into the community concerning these meetings, and soon there were thirty to forty people in attendance. She searched for the most impressive sermons she could find and read them to her gathering of hungry hearts. Soon, the attendance grew to standing room only—about two hundred people.

Susanna also began meeting individually with her children to determine the condition of their souls and their commitment to God.

Susanna informed Samuel about the meetings in a letter, and Samuel responded, expressing many concerns. He was unsure they should continue. Susanna wrote back in a very straightforward manner, going head-to-head with each one of his arguments with clarity and humility. Then Samuel gave his approval, and the meetings continued, enabling both the family and community to experience the grace of God together.

Stop the Meetings

Susanna's success unleashed the fury anger and jealousy of the curate, Mr. Inman. He wrote a letter to Samuel, accusing Susanna of holding illegal religious meetings. Afraid her gatherings would bring disapproval from the church and ruin his future ministerial career, Samuel changed his stance and asked Susanna to stop the meetings. Susanna's reply to this latest challenge is worthy of quoting, at least in part:

> I shall not inquire how it was possible that you should be prevailed on by the senseless clamors of two or three of the worst of your parish, to condemn

what you so lately approved....It is plain in fact that this one thing has brought more people to church that ever anything did in so short a time. We used not to have above twenty to twenty-five at evening service, whereas we have now between two and three hundred; which are more than ever came before to hear Inman in the morning....Now, I beseech you, weigh all these things in an impartial balance: on the one side, the honor of almighty God, the doing much good to many souls, and the friendship of the best among whom we live; on the other, the senseless objections of a few scandalous persons...and when you have duly considered all things, let me have your positive determination....If you do, after all, think fit to dissolve this assembly, do not tell me that you desire me to do it, for that will not satisfy my conscience; but send me your positive command, in such full and express terms as may absolve me from all guilt and punishment, for neglecting this opportunity of doing good, when you and I shall appear before the great and awful tribunal of our Lord Jesus Christ.[1]

Fire was burning in her soul, but wisdom kept her on sound footing. There is no record of Samuel writing back to command that Susanna stop the meetings. They continued until he returned home.

Samuel reaped great benefit from his wife's efforts. His children were being spiritually nurtured. His parish was growing considerably in attendance and in the grace of God.

Neighbors who before had fired their guns off in front of his home and who probably had been responsible for setting his home on fire were now supporting them for the first time. The most important benefit of all was that the form and structure of Susanna's meetings would eventually make up the basis for the entire Methodist movement. God lit a fire in Susanna's soul that would eventually ignite many souls around the world.

All this was accomplished by one woman's commitment to nurturing in her children a love for God. She achieved a delicate balance of walking within the boundaries of the cultural understanding about women's roles while daring to step out and do something radical. While honoring her husband and submitting herself to him, she was confident enough to do what had never been done before, braving great criticism.

An Innovator and Educator

Susanna was also an energetic innovator in education. She believed that all children, girls as well as boys, should receive a good education that included religious training, and she was convinced that the only way she could be sure it would happen was to do it herself. She developed extensive teaching manuals, including three theological manuals, the first of which discussed the order and design of creation and how it testified to God's existence. The second manual dealt with the great doctrines of the Christian faith using the Apostles' Creed, and the third expounded upon the Ten Commandments, teaching the major tenets of divine moral law. She also wrote many theologically instructive letters to her children.

Susanna ordered her children's daily schedule strictly. She believed that bringing a child's will into respectful subjection to their parents and to God was the key to nurturing their spirits. Her lessons were consistently undergirded by her love and devotion, and the Wesley children excelled under her loving instruction.

Susanna's writings concerned salvation and every theological concern. She wrote concerning the sin of the will, the sin of the imagination, the sin of the memory, the sin of the passions of the soul, summing it up by writing that "sin is the greatest contradiction imaginable to his most holy nature."[2]

About God, she wrote of His "infinite purity, absolutely separated from all moral imperfection."[3] "He is goodness, and his most holy will cannot swerve or decline from what is so. He always wills what is absolutely best; nor can he possibly be deceived or deceive anyone."[4] "But the infinite goodness of God, who delights that his mercy should triumph over justice, though he provided no remedy for the fallen angels, yet man being a more simple kind of creature, who perhaps did not sin so maliciously against so much knowledge as those apostate spirits did, he would not subject the whole race of mankind to be ruined and destroyed by the fraud and subtlety of Satan; but he gave us help by one who was mighty, that is able and willing to save to the uttermost all such as shall come to God through him."[5]

Through her children, especially John and Charles and their Methodist movement, Susanna touched the entire world. Her message of devotion to God and hunger to see lost souls come to God was much needed in the society of eighteenth-century England, where true religious conviction had become a rare commodity. Reason was exalted above the Bible, and Christianity was reduced to a code of ethics. Nearly lost was the understanding that sin must be forgiven and cleansed by a miracle-working God who had become man and died on a cross.

Passing Down the Seed of Spiritual Desire

In 1728, Charles experienced an awakening in the Spirit while he and John were attending Oxford University. He began praying and ministering to the sick and needy, and eventually formed what was called the Holy Club, later known as the Methodist Society. John joined the group and became a leader within this new movement.

John and Susanna exchanged many letters discussing doctrinal issues. She helped him formulate the foundation stones for the Methodism. Convinced that the gospel message could transform society, John built on what he had experienced under his mother's tutelage, advocating a methodical expression of devotion and frequent meetings with other believers. Eventually, he also promoted lay preaching and teaching, which are still part of the Methodist church today.

On May 21, 1738, Charles attended a meeting with the Moravian Society, a fiery evangelistic group that preached justification by faith alone. This meeting was a life-changing experience.[6] During this meeting, God touched Charles and he received an assurance of his salvation.

Three days later, in what has become known as his Aldersgate Street experience, John had a similar encounter with the same Moravian Society. He wrote his now-famous words: "I felt my heart strangely warmed. I felt I did trust in Christ, Christ alone for salvation; and an assurance was given me that he had taken away my sins, even mine, and saved me from the law of sin and death."[7]

John had been ordained as a minister in the Church of England but was expelled because of his "fanatic" ideas. So, he took to the streets and open fields, preaching wherever people would listen. As a result, many people came to Christ. He opened a free medical dispensary in 1746 and spent much of his time visiting the sick, ministering to the poor, and preaching to masses of people. "The world is my parish" expressed John's heart well.

By the end of his life, Charles became known as one of the greatest hymn writers in the world, writing the words to over six thousand hymns. Most of his clearly articulated, theologically sound hymns continue to be sung today. The Methodist revival, led by John and Charles Wesley, transformed church life in both Britain and the American colonies, and gave rise to much-needed social reform. By the grace of God, Susanna's influence for the kingdom of God reached the ends of the earth.

Susanna faithfully loved God and served Him every way she knew how. She saw the vital importance of developing a thoroughly biblical foundation for one's life, and she believed that everyone needed to search the heart regularly and confess sins to God. She was a person "in process," just as we all are, who did not receive a revelation of the assurance of her salvation until later in life, but that did not stop her from pursuing her secret place in God.

After Samuel's death in 1735, Susanna was compelled to live with her adult children in turn. She had made her peace with her many losses and privations, and she made herself a welcome addition to their households. When she herself was at death's doorstep, she asked her children to sing a psalm of praise to God at her funeral.

The following words were inscribed on the tombstone of this great lover of God:

> Here lies the body of Mrs. Susanna Wesley,
> the youngest and last surviving daughter
> of Dr. Samuel Annesley.
> In sure and steadfast hope to rise
> And claim her mansion in the skies,
> A Christian here her flesh laid down,
> The cross exchanging for a crown.
> True daughter of affliction, she,
> Inured to pain and misery,
> Mourn'd a long night of griefs and fears,
> A legal night of seventy years:
> The Father then reveal'd his son,
> Him in the broken bread made known;
> She knew and felt her sins forgiven,
> And found the earnest of heaven.
> Meet for the fellowship above,
> She heard the call, "Arise, my love."

"I come," her dying looks replied,
And lamblike, as her Lord, she died.[8]

Years later, her tombstone was changed to reflect her faithfulness to her husband and respect for her sons, John and Charles.

> Here lies the body of
> MRS. SUSANNA WESLEY,
> Widow of the Rev. Samuel Wesley, M.A.
> (late Rector of Epworth, in Lincolnshire,)
> who died July 23, 1742,
> aged 73 years.
> She was the youngest daughter of the
> Rev. Samuel Annesley, D.D.
> Ejected by the Act of Uniformity
> From the Rectory of St. Giles's,
> Cripplegate, August 24, 1662.
> She was the mother of nineteen children,
> Of whom the most eminent were the
> REV. JOHN WESLEY AND CHARLES WESLEY;
> The former of whom was under God the
> Founder of the Societies of the People
> Called Methodists.[9]

Surely, her secret place with God had been her most treasured place. She wrote:

My joys all center in him, and it is he himself that I desire; it is his favor, it is his acceptance, the communications of his grace, that I earnestly wish for more than anything in the world; and I have no relish or delight in anything when under apprehensions of his displeasure. I rejoice in my relationship to him, that he is my Father, my Lord, my God. I rejoice that he has power over me, and I desire to live in subjection to him; that he condescends to punish me when I transgress his laws, as a father chastens the son whom he loves. I thank him that he has brought me thus far; and I will beware of despairing of his mercy for the time which is yet to come, but will give God the glory of his free grace.[10]

Make this prayer of Susanna Wesley's your own:

Help me, O Lord, to make true use of all disappointments and calamities in this life, in such a way that they may unite my heart more closely with you. Cause them to separate my affections from worldly things and inspire my soul with more vigor in the pursuit of true happiness. Until this temper of mind be attained, I can never enjoy any settled peace, much less a calm serenity. You only, O God, can satisfy my immortal soul and bestow those spiritual pleasures that alone are proper to its nature. Grant me grace to stay and center my soul in you; to confine its desire, hopes, and expectations of happiness to you alone; calmly to attend to the seasons of your providence and to have a firm, habitual resignation to your will. Enable me to love you, my God, with all my heart, with all my mind, with all my strength; so to love you as to desire you; so to desire you as to be uneasy without you, without your favor, without some such resemblance to you as my nature in this imperfect state can bear. Amen.[11]

—✝—

Chapter Seven

Basilea Schlink *(1904–2001):*

GOD SENT
ME TO THE CROSS

At the same time that Basilea Schlink was setting out to discover the world as a young woman, Hitler's influence was beginning to emerge within Germany. She began her studies in social welfare in 1923, while Hitler was attempting his first revolution, which severely shook the economy, causing inflation and bread rationing. Even as her nation was shaken to the core by political upheaval, Basilea's heart experienced its own kind of unrest, as she came to grips with interior issues of true humility and repentance from sin, pride, and ambition.

She stated, "In my childhood and early youth it was always the same. When my sinful nature sought satisfaction, God sent me a cross so that a part of me had to die."[1]

Born in Darmstadt, Germany, on October 21, 1904,

Basilea's heart from an early age was turned toward the Lord. Although she was high-spirited and enjoyed as many activities as other girls of her age, the call of God echoed deep in her soul. At the age of twenty, Basilea's prayer was, "Preserve this inner life, but take away my self-esteem. All that I have comes from You and all the good in me can only be attributed to You, Lord Jesus. That I know very well."[2]

As a young woman, Basilea longed for someone to lead her to God. Finding no one, she worked hard to improve herself. Living without the transforming power of God soon brought her to the end of her striving. She realized she needed a revelation of God in her heart. In August 1922, God answered her plea and she beheld Jesus inwardly as the crucified Lord. She knew that she had come into the saving knowledge of Jesus Christ

Revelation of the Father's love began to flow into her. The mystery of the grace of God unfolded in her heart, and her self-effort fell away as she yearned to discover how to pray and grow in God's love. Jesus Himself led her and taught her. When she became aware that a particular activity that brought her pleasure actually grieved the Holy Spirit, she let go of that thing out of love for Him.

Treasures of the Heart

God deposited many treasures into Basilea's heart as she matured into adulthood. She learned that God would reveal Himself to her to the extent that she would allow His Word to convict her heart. God spoke to her of the need to come to the end of self and to walk in repentance so that the death that sin produces would be broken off and new life would result. She experienced greater dimensions of His love, and her heart became increasingly sensitive to the things that God values.

The purifying process continued in Basilea as the Lord brought His light to the motives of her heart. Why did she want to help people? Was she giving them God's love—or *her* love? She was learning how important it is to love people with divine love, because human love is impure and limited. Divine love is constant and sure; it does not waiver with the ebb and flow of human emotions and circumstances. Basilea learned how to give Him the highest place not because of any desire to minister to others, but because of love for Him alone.

Like Peeling an Onion

During her university years, as she completed her studies and then turned to teaching, she experienced mountain peaks and valleys with the Lord. At times she felt very alone. It seemed that God was silently asking her, *Am I enough for you even when it feels like I'm dead, even when I do not give you inner consolation or loving proofs of My presence?*[3]

As Basilea allowed the Lord's piercing question go deep into her spirit, she was convicted of her sin and she asked for His forgiveness. He transformed her heart to experience true thankfulness, and gratitude for His goodness and faithfulness spilled over from her soul.

Like peeling the skin of an onion, He was dealing with issues of her heart, layer by layer, exposing darkness she didn't even know was there. His great love and compassion were exposing darkness of the soul and bringing her to the light. She was learning that in the valleys, in dark and lonely places, was where His glorious light could shine the very brightest.

In 1930 Basilea attended the university in Berlin to work on her Ph.D. in psychology. She lived part of this time with her friend Erika, and she began to feel that God planned for the two of them to found and build up a ministry. During this time also, Basilea felt convicted to live a celibate life.

In 1933, at the height of Nazi National Socialism, Basilea's Jewish professors were forced to relinquish their positions. From 1933 to 1935, this young student held the position of national president of the Women's Division of the German Student Christian Movement. As part of the government-resisting Confessing Church, Basilea was used to influence the Christian student group to reject a paragraph stating that only German (Aryan) girls would be permitted to attend the meetings. The fact that Hebrew Christian students would continue to be accepted within these circles meant that their entire organization could be dissolved. Basilea was beginning to step out in courageous faith to stand up for the Jewish people under the Nazis.

Frontline Courage

Trials, poverty, and hardships followed in the years from 1936 to 1938. Basilea and Erika moved to Darmstadt, where they felt they were to begin a Bible training course for women who were to become pastors' wives or go into ministry themselves. With no way of earning a living, the two young women trusted God for every need. They lived in real poverty, and dug into God for their continual sustenance and spiritual development. By the end of the second year, a handful of women had completed their course.

By the fall of 1938, with no money and no women registering for their course, it seemed the dream had died. But at the last moment, a couple of local pastors pulled together some financial aid to help fund youth work. Basilea started a girls' youth ministry, which quickly grew to a hundred members under Erika's leadership. Basilea was by then in her mid-thirties, still without a clear ministry.

In 1939, the Missionary Society for Moslems asked Basilea to take over its traveling lectureship. So, during the desperate, difficult years of war throughout Europe, Basilea traveled in crowded trains, enduring blackouts, severe coal shortages, and bombing raids. In the frigid winter of 1940–1941, she traveled for four weeks across Prussia, where the temperatures often sank below zero. Wherever she went, she found that God was her faithful and constant companion, her security, and her peace.

Sometimes informers were present in her meetings, but she continued to feel compelled to speak of God's plan of salvation for the Jews, and of His special covenant with them. Twice she was reported by these informants and interrogated for hours by the secret police. Still, God kept her safe and she was not arrested. Her Bible studies were allowed to continue even though both the Old and New Testaments were taught, which was forbidden under Hitler.

As Basilea traveled from place to place, she spoke on the power of Jesus' blood, His victory over the enemy, and His triumphant return. She covered Jesus' second coming, God's plan of salvation for Israel and the city of God, heaven and hell, the blessings of suffering, and how to overcome.

For years, she prayed, "Grant me love, love which is not irritable or resentful, which bears all things, hopes all things, believes all things, endures all things."[4] In part through her experiences during World War II, God taught her the way of humility. She learned to cease from self-justification and to endure with patience and forbearance. God's perfect love became her life's message.

Revival

On September 11, 1944, an air raid targeted Darmstadt. Buildings were toppled everywhere. Yet this black cloud contained a silver lining. It so sobered the girls with whom Erika and Basilea had been working that revival was unleashed. These young women were seized with the intense need for personal repentance. And as they spent extra time in prayer, the Lord dealt with the two leaders concerning the sins of their nation.

During the war years, Basilea and Erika had spent time in prayer over personal issues, but they realized they had not cried out for national sins, nor had they repented for the prisoners of war and for the millions of Jews who had been slaughtered. They had thought they were devoting their lives to God, but had they seen their lives in light of the sin of their nation? Great conviction fell upon the ashes of Darmstadt, and from that, great revival.

The stage was being set for the foundation of one of Basilea's dreams—the Evangelical Sisterhood of Mary.

The Evangelical Sisterhood of Mary

On March 30, 1947, the dream became a reality. The Sisterhood was established, founded by Basilea Schlink and Paul Riedinger, a Methodist church leader. It had Lutheran roots, but eventually it became interdenominational. In the early days, they weathered criticism, lacks, and sickness, but they grew steadily to become a community of women living in an attitude of contrition and fellowship in bridal love for Jesus. The Sisters of Mary would stand in the gap for their nation, identifying Germany's sins as their own and crying out for mercy and forgiveness.

Often, Basilea retreated into seclusion with God. She spent weeks rarely seeing or talking to anyone. During such times she experienced the sweet presence of God and the sense of eternity resting in her room. In times of seclusion, she received revelations from God concerning His nature or the Scripture. Many times He would direct her into serious assignments that would take much prayer to be accomplished.

The Sufferings of Jesus

Basilea gained understanding into the sufferings of Jesus, and she learned that loneliness is one of the ways He suffered while here on earth. The Lord would come to her in those times and share burdens of His heart with her. He spoke to her of His pain that the body of Christ was not unified. This sent her on many missions to build up and repair the breach, in an attitude of humility and repentance, asking for forgiveness. She was often met with divisive words, but sometimes true reconciliation took place. She was a true forerunner, one who not only understood the power and importance of what we call "identificational repentance," but who actually practiced it.

In May 1949, Mother Basilea (as she was called) felt inspired to build a chapel for Jesus, where He would be adored. The Sisters of Mary also needed a house where new sisters could join the ministry. When they started these projects, they had only thirty German marks. It seemed that the Lord was serving as their banker. Both buildings were completed in a timely fashion; the chapel was built from bricks salvaged from the ruins of the city. This home for the Evangelical Sisterhood of Mary became known as Kanaan.

During one of her times of seclusion, Mother Basilea received a commission from God to speak to the Pope. She was to go and discuss God's desire for all His body to become one. Specifically, she would discuss the breach between Protestants and Roman Catholics.

Before she could go, she knew that much work would need to be completed. She knew that the enemy's attacks always correspond to the spiritual significance of the commission. She had learned to identify with the words of Paul: "Now I rejoice in my sufferings on your behalf. And with my own body I supplement whatever is lacking [on our part] of Christ's afflictions, on behalf of His body, which is the church" (Col. 1:24, AMP). Mother Basilea learned to suffer for the unity of love. The inner conflicts she endured were an essential part of preparing for this assignment, so she repented of faultfinding and personal opinions and submitted her mind anew to the lordship of Jesus.

Through prayer, she was able to attain a private audience with Pope Pius XII. Her assignment was fulfilled. She could not determine his response, but she had faithfully answered God's call to be a voice echoing the ache in God's heart. The pope responded to her, "Is that really the Savior's wish?"[5]

Mother Basilea knew that the seeds we are asked to sow take time to germinate and we cannot guarantee when the fruit will become evident. We sowers must be patient and always carry an eternal perspective, with plenty of faith that *God's seeds always grow.*

After her trip to Rome, the Evangelical Sisterhood of Mary opened up branches in England, Greece, and Italy. The work crossed denominational borders into the Anglican, Greek Orthodox, and Roman Catholic churches. Eventually, branches included more than two hundred women from twenty countries, along with fourteen men in the Canaan Franciscan Brothers.

God's Heart for Israel

In other times of seclusion beginning in 1954, God spoke to Mother Basilea about His heart for Israel, His specially chosen people. A cry for God's people arose from her heart toward the throne of mercy: "Awaken souls amongst Your chosen people Israel to love You like a bride so that one day they may be with You in the City of God."[6]

With this call came the realization that Germany, Basilea's homeland, had committed horrible atrocities against the Jewish people and by doing so, they had heaped terrible guilt upon themselves. As she entered into specific times of prayer and fasting concerning this overpowering weight of sin, the light of God broke through. No longer did the sisters avoid houses they knew belonged to Jewish families because of guilt or shame. With God's renewed love in their hearts, they visited these families, asking for forgiveness on behalf of their nation. Repentance began to do the work of reconciliation.

When the sisters desired to visit Israel, an invitation was required in order to issue visas because of their German citizenship. The door was opened; an invitation came to the doorstep. They obtained the necessary visas and walked through the land of Israel, asking God's forgiveness for Germany's sin. Their labors toward reconciliation resulted in sending two sisters to live there in 1957. Mother Basilea went on to write a book calling Christians to an awareness of its sins against the Jews.

Later, an additional branch of the Sisters of Mary was established in Jerusalem, called Beth Abraham. These events brought invitations from Jewish communities within the United States and Canada for Mother Basilea to speak in their synagogues. Rabbis and students attended her meetings.

The Valley of the Shadow of Death

In 1959, Mother Basilea was suffering from a serious heart condition. Inwardly, she felt she was being led through the valley of the shadow of death. After releasing her will into God's will for her life, she received an assurance from God that she would recover. The Lord granted health to her, and she became stronger than before. Soon after this trial, she wrote the book *Repentance—The Joy-Filled Life* (Bethany House, 1984). She understood that "a person lacking contrition lacks everything. If he has contrition and repentance, he has everything he needs, for repentance draws down God's grace."[7]

In 1959 came another call from God concerning the land of Israel. Mother Basilea was to spend time in the Holy Land seeking out the places where Jesus had lived and suffered in order to pray for an awakening of God's purposes for those places. As she traveled through the land, she felt the grief of Jesus Christ, because His people remained so unmoved toward the places where He had lived His earthly life and so little was being done to keep those sights holy.

She spent time in prayer in Gethsemane at Lithostrotos, where Christ was crowned with thorns, and at the Kidron Valley, where He was led away as a prisoner. Here she experienced a living encounter with God and wrote many songs, devotional readings, and texts. She compiled these writings into books for pilgrims visiting these sites. Booklets and leaflets were created from her book and distributed by the thousands at the holy sites, as well as given away at various hotels. After this, the Sisters of Mary began hosting spiritual pilgrimages of the Holy Land.

A few years later, the Sisters were permitted to place plaques at the holy sites. Each one was inscribed with devotional thoughts to help visitors open their hearts to God in these places.

Memorials to God's Glory

After the enthusiastic success of the memorial plaques in Israel, Mother Basilea and her sisters began praying about a new project in their home country of Germany. The Sisters of Mary sought permission to erect plaques at various scenic points to bring glory to God. After the plaques were erected, stories were told of many individuals who were kept from committing suicide because of their presence. Eventually, this project became an international effort, with plaques being placed at points of majestic beauty in many nations.

Mother Basilea accomplished many things during her lifetime, much more than can be accounted for here. Throughout her life, her primary goal was to love Jesus and to call others to love Him as our wonderful Bridegroom should be loved. Her many written works resulted from this devotion in her heart for Him. The effects of her love and devotion continue to bless those in many nations.

Mother Basilea went to be with the Lord on March 21, 2001, but her work and vision for the Evangelical Sisterhood of Mary continues. This community is dedicated to Christian radio ministry and to Christian literature. The Sisterhood publishes tracts in ninety languages, which are distributed on five continents. Radio and television programs are broadcast in twenty-three languages. But more important than the programs and other efforts is the fire of His love and the call to the secret place.

That privileged cry continues to echo across generations and ages of time. Let's turn now to hear its message to our own generation through the lives of those who have cultivated blessed friendship in the secret place.

Our Savior, You are the only one worth living for! Like Mother Basilea, I offer myself to You entirely and freely, trusting that You will form Your desires in my heart and use me in whatever ways You choose. Teach me Your eternal perspective and show me how to carry Your love wherever You may send me. Very few of us are called as part of a band of women like the Sisterhood, but we are all called as part of Your body, the Church, to spread the fragrance of Your gracious presence everywhere, driving out darkness with Your radiant light. Always in Jesus' name, amen.

Part Three

Friends of the Secret Place

Chapter Eight

Gwen Shaw *(1924–2013)*

A PASSION FOR NATIONS

G wen Shaw ministered in more than one hundred nations and was the founder of the End-Time Handmaidens, an organization that has lit the pathway to the secret place for nearly a generation. She was truly born to serve the Lord, and it was an honor and a joy to be her friend.

Loving and serving her Lord was her destiny. Gwendolyn Ruth had parents who dedicated her to the Lord from the womb. Gwen's mother came from a godly family of sincere Mennonites who had served the Lord for many generations. Her God-fearing forefathers had paid a terrible price for their testimony.

Years earlier, these new believers had been banished from their beautiful homes in the Emmental Valley of the Swiss Alps because of their conviction that salvation was by grace alone. The teachings of Martin Luther had swept across Europe and many of the faithful had died as martyrs, being burned at the stake or speared through. Young men were sold as galley slaves, and old fathers were left to die in dark dungeons. Gwen's ancestors had been forced to leave their homes and live a life of wandering for decades until Russia opened its doors. There they found religious freedom.[1]

During the first bitter Russian winter in their new homeland, they existed by digging holes in the ground and living under the earth. Gradually, they began to raise crops and prosper until they finally owned their own homes. Towns and villages of German-speaking people, all of them seeking religious freedom, arrived in Russia.[2]

When all seemed to be going well, the Lord visited His people and warned them through the gift of prophecy that great persecution was coming to Russia. This persecution would be greater than any they had ever known in the past, and for those who stayed, there would be no survivors. God told them to leave Russia and go to a new homeland. Some heeded the word of the Lord, while others mocked it and stayed behind where, sadly, they suffered and died.

This is how Gwen came to be born in Canada. As a young man, her maternal grandfather, Peter Miller (Mueller) and others traveled to Canada in obedience to the word of the Lord. These hardworking farmers grew hearty wheat from the grain that they had brought with them from Russia.[3] They founded churches and raised families. Gwen grew up attending the Emmanuel Mennonite Church, which had been founded by her grandfather in Saskatchewan, the middle prairie province of Canada. Here her parents dedicated their three children—Gwen, Earl, and Jamie—to the Lord. The entire family faithfully attended the church built on the land dedicated by Grandfather Miller.

In her middle teens, Gwen grew bored with rural prairie life and escaped with a friend to the big city. While she was away, her family was dramatically touched by the Pentecostal movement sweeping through the community. Meanwhile, Gwen was part of a more liberal congregation where sin was seldom mentioned and people felt free to live any way they wanted.

After a few months of rebellion and desperate prayers by her family, Gwen came back to the Lord and was gloriously filled with the Holy Spirit. She went off to the Assembly of God (Pentecostal Assembly of Canada) Bible School in Ontario to be trained for the Lord's work.

While she was there, revival fire fell among the students; visions, spiritual gifts, intercession, and deep conviction of the Lord's presence flowed freely during those special days. In the midst of this outpouring, God called Gwen to China. However, somewhat ignorantly, Gwen had married a young man who was not as fervent about God's purposes. Gwen prayed and prayed. Eventually, the Lord moved on his heart, and in obedience they went off as faith missionaries to China.

Launching Out Into the Deep

In December 1947, they landed in Shanghai. Gwen had just turned twenty-three. Having responded in obedience to the call of God upon her life, she received a passionate burden from the Lord for the Chinese people.

Sometimes that burden was greater than at other times. As the years went by and China fell into the hands of Communism, the doors for the gospel in Mainland China slammed shut. Even so, Gwen continued to serve the Lord among the Chinese people in Taiwan and Hong Kong, not missing a step in fulfilling that call of God. Never for a moment did she think of turning back from that call.

Gwen loved the Chinese, and she considered them her people. She shared, "I belonged to them, and their need was my need; their pain, my pain."[4] In fact, Gwen had been God's spokeswoman, used to warn and foretell the closing of the nation of China to missionary work long before it ever fell to the Communists.[5] The prophetic utterance doubtless fueled the flame of passion within her heart, and the Canadian volunteer reached out to China with a deep sense of urgency.

After ten years of marriage on the mission field, three sons arrived: David, Danny, and Tommy. As a mother of young children, Gwen's life was now occupied with family affairs. She admitted later that it was hard to be a mother of three lively boys and still keep her missionary vision alive. But with the help of an *amah* (housemaid and nanny), the boys' early years were spent growing up on the mission field in Hong Kong.

One day in 1963, after sixteen years of missionary service, God met her with a new and wonderful anointing. Fresh desire arose in her heart. Gwen hungered for more of God, and she longed for her life to make a difference. Dedicating her life afresh to God, Gwen determined that from that point on it would be 100 percent, complete, unconditional, and total surrender to His will—whatever the cost. And God took her up on the vow she had made to Him.

Fresh Anointing—Renewed Vision

With God's renewal of His calling in Gwen's life, Gwen followed, adding to her mission field the nations of the world. She never imagined all that God had planned for her. "I simply put my hand in His and began to follow Him step-by-step, day-by-day, and nation by nation."[6] She also never anticipated the great cost of her obedience—difficulties that would fix her eyes completely on Jesus, the Lover of her soul.

With this new "double-portion" anointing came a tremendous burden for souls and an overwhelming vision for the nations. Her fresh call took her to various parts of China, Mongolia, Taiwan, the Philippines, and on to Indonesia, where she saw the Lord do great miracles of deliverance and salvation. She would minister among the Presbyterians in one location, the Pentecostal Assemblies in another, and with Catholic nuns and Orthodox priests. She came alongside the Methodists, Baptists, Missionary Alliance, Salvation Army—whoever was hungry for more of God. Wherever the Spirit said, "Come," Sister Gwen went.

During the children's summer vacation, Gwen often would take one of them with her when she went to minister. Nine-year-old David, the oldest, played the trumpet and always knew how to get a crowd. He would borrow someone's bicycle, ride out to the marketplace, and play his trumpet while passing out tracts and flyers about the meetings. Turning toward the gathering, he would encourage them to come and hear his mother preach. They had great times together.

The Terrible Price

On other occasions when the children were in school, Gwen went out alone. Long before this time, she and her husband had grown apart in vision and calling, and this had resulted in a painful separation of ways. The Lord used this pain redemptively as a part of a breaking process in which He took Gwen into a deeper place where He alone became her husband, shelter, and refuge.

At times Gwen's loneliness became so acute that it pierced into her heart like a knife. Only God knew her tears, pain, loneliness, and longing—the price she paid to fulfill her vow to God.

At one point, she started to make excuses to try to escape God's call, and she nearly lost all three of her boys. Danny almost drowned in the South China Sea; David slipped right in front of a fast oncoming car; and Tommy was miraculously rescued out of a sewage-filled river. Still, the Lord promised His fatherly protection if she would only keep following Him.

Gwen knew that God was speaking loud and clear, warning her of how costly it could be to put anything before Him—even her children. The price might be more costly than the one she was already paying. So again, she counted the cost and said yes to her Lord. That's when she received her next assignment—India.

India, "My Great Love"

India became Gwen's great love. She often would say, "China was my first love, and India was my great love."[7] She couldn't find words to describe what it meant to feel God's heartbeat of love for a nation. She would have gladly laid down her whole life for the Lord in India. In fact, that became her desire.

In this season of her life, she experienced great joy in service to God. She traveled to many parts of northern India, erected a tent, and openly preached the gospel of the Lord Jesus Christ. She was a woman on the front lines. What joy to see people respond to the mercy of God! How exciting to lead many Hindus and Muslims to Jesus!

Gwen translated her tract called *Who Is Jesus?* into the Bengali language and used it as she ministered from Punjab to Calcutta, New Delhi to Allahabad, and from coast to coast.[8] Her father and brother joined her in those harvest fields of souls under the big tent. Gwen played an accordion and brother Earl joined her in singing songs of Zion. Revival was in the air.

After India, Gwen moved on to Russia, and once again God's heart of passion for the lost beat inside her as if it were her own. Miraculously, she was the first woman to preach in the Baptist Church in Moscow. Like the apostolic ambassadors of old, Gwen would pray, fast, and agonize for the nations. When no door was open to her, God would be the door. When no finances existed, He would be her provider.

Jesus became the doorkeeper of the nations, opening entry to Finland, Bali, Denmark, Norway, Sweden, England, Germany, Africa, Pakistan, the United States, and Canada. If she could pronounce it, Jesus took this little Canadian lady there. He introduced her to kings and princesses, paupers and lepers, and she shared with all the timeless story of God's great grace and wonderful love.

Argentina, the Founding of the End-Time Handmaidens

If God's love is in your heart, then your heart will expand to be like His. This is just what happened in Sister Gwen. How much can one heart contain? Remember, "For God so loved the world…" (John 3:16).

Her next call came and she went to Argentina, where once again she felt the heartbeat of God, now for the Spanish-speaking people of that great land. Throughout Argentina, she saw the mighty hand of God working with mighty displays of supernatural power following her preaching of His Word.

Then one night in Buenos Aires, something happened that was destined to change many lives. Gwen had just ministered in a large Assembly of God church where God had poured out His Spirit. Miracles of healing had taken place, and people had seen angels. God's tangible presence had manifested among them. No one wanted to leave the meetings as the God of the secret place was being revealed so openly.

Gwen went back tired and exhausted to her lonely hotel room that night, and lay there on her bed. Looking up to heaven, she asked God questions. "God, how can you use me? Why do you use me? I am nothing. I make mistakes. I am far from perfect. Yet I have seen your glory like a trail of fire following me everywhere. How? Why?"

Amazingly, she heard His answer: "It is because you are willing to do anything I ask you to do!"

With the curiosity of a child, Gwen inquired, "Is that all, Lord? Then You could use anyone, any woman who like myself would be totally surrendered to You!"

"Yes, My child, I could," He answered.

Strengthened in faith, Gwen responded, "Then, Lord, raise up ten thousand women—women just like myself who will pay any price, make any sacrifice, and be totally obedient to Your will."[9] The year was 1966.

The End of the Road

Four years later, after she had ministered in many other nations all over the world, Gwen found herself in Chicago, seemingly at the end of the road. Her children were in Hong Kong. Her marriage was over. Her heart was broken, and she was sure that she could never serve God again. Her emotions overwhelmed her as the enemy whispered that no one would accept a woman whose marriage had fallen apart.

Gwen underwent a twenty-one-day fast and waited upon the Lord. "I did the only thing I knew to do. I went back to the drawing board, back to the Cross."[11] He spoke to her again. Night after night the Lord came to her releasing His plans, visiting her by His angels, answering her questions.

To confirm these encounters, the Lord of Hosts sent a prophet to tell her that she must begin to call out the End-Time Handmaidens. God told her that there was an army of women out there in the background, standing "idle in the marketplace, whom no one had hired." They were waiting to hear the call to go out and serve the Lord in the harvest fields of the world.

Perhaps no one knew those harvest fields better than Sister Gwen. Already, she had been to many of the nations of the world. Although she had been thinking, *It's all over*, God was revealing that it was not.

The Beginning of a New Calling

With fresh resolve and faith, in obedience Gwen began to give the call to women everywhere to join her in sharing her burden for souls. A new and living company of women was born— one full of consecration, holiness, and the Word of the Lord. The End-Time Handmaidens rose up from many nations as the Holy Spirit prepared women's hearts around the world in the same way He had prepared hers. God's chosen daughters would fast and pray, in brokenness wondering if God even knew their names. Then, from the stillness in His wonderful presence, He would call their names. A growing number of End-Time Handmaidens were commissioned into the harvest, radiating the glow of holiness from the secret place.

The Lord did not forget his handmaiden Gwen. He sent to her a "Simon" to help her carry the cross and lighten the load. At a time of fellowship in Santa Barbara, California, Gwen met Lieutenant Colonel James von Doornum Shaw, a retired Baptist US Air Force pilot.

When she saw him, the Holy Spirit told her to go and lay hands upon this stranger and prophesy to him. Reluctantly, she obeyed and declared to this Baptist man that God was bringing him into a new consecration and that times of satisfaction and joy from the Holy Spirit were waiting for him like none he had never known. She declared that as he had flown in the natural, so would he fly in the spiritual realm. Gwen spoke the word "completeness" over this man.

Jim Shaw went on a fast to seek the face of the Lord, and a new heart for missions bubbled up in him. Little did Gwen realize that she would end up marrying this wonderful man who had flown numerous aircraft for well over thirty years and that together they would fly to many nations, serving the Lord. The End-Time Handmaidens would also become complete by adding the male component, End-Time Servants, as well, and that they would serve the Master together for another thirty years.

Looking Back

Gwen first gave her heart to the Lord when she was seventeen years old, and since then she has served Him with all her heart. In her words:

> If I could live my life over again, I would give it all to God again. God has given me supernatural strength to fulfill a supernatural calling. But, as hard as I

work and as fast as I run, I can't keep up with Him. I have now been to over one hundred nations and still they keep calling. Day after day they're calling, calling, calling. This call to the nations is there, ringing in my ears, burning in my heart. I want to go, but I'm getting older now. I can't preach four and five times a day as I used to in Indonesia. I can understand the heart's cry of Moses when he said, "I am not able to bear all this people alone, because it is too heavy for me." (Num. 11:14, KJV)

Yes, it is getting too heavy for me. This terrible burden for Cambodia, North Korea, Tibet, Zambia, Pakistan, Albania, Chile, Iceland, and all the nations where I have not yet told the old, old story of Jesus and His love—besides the nations where I want to return again! Moses wept. I weep too!

Then I hear God say to me what He said to Moses, "I will take of the spirit which is upon thee, and will put it upon them; and they shall bear the burden of the people with thee, that thou bear it not thyself alone." (Num. 11:17b, KJV)[11]

Sharing Her Burden

When God calls people in the same way He called Gwen Shaw, He sovereignly and supernaturally places a burden on their hearts. If they are willing to accept it, they must recognize that it will not be easy. Following the call will cost everything. Like the tribe of Levi, which had no earthly inheritance, the Lord must be their inheritance.

Total, unconditional surrender to the glorious Father of the Lord Jesus Christ can be expressed by praying the following prayer, composed by Gwen Shaw:

Lord, I give myself to You. I give my life to You. I feel Your call. I believe I was sent to do the will of my Father. I will take orders from You.

I will submit to You. I will let You break my will. I will not seek for comfort nor high position, nor do what I want to do. I love You, Jesus; I thank You for calling me, and I am grateful that you want me, and that You can use me.

All I can say is, "Send the fire and burn up the sacrifice. Fill me with Thy Holy Spirit and give me a double portion of Thine anointing."[12]

Chapter Nine

✝

Elizabeth Alves

THE GRANDMA OF THE PRAYER SHIELD

never wanted a ministry. All I ever wanted was to know Christ!" These words epitomize the heart and motive of another intimate friend of the secret place, Elizabeth (Beth) Alves.

When you're sitting in a meeting listening to Beth speak, you might easily feel as though you have been ushered into her living room. Her mothering grace is calm and unassuming. Here is a woman who has traveled to over thirty nations, faithfully bringing the life of Christ to others, rich or poor. Beth Alves exudes the love of God, and she knows that all her accomplishments are not really hers, but His.

Beth and her late husband, Floyd, began the early years of their marriage in the Lutheran church. In Beth's words, they were Lutherans first and Christians second. But God didn't let it stay that way.

Power From on High

Beth remembers the pivotal time within her family that was key to their spiritual awakening. Her daughter had been diagnosed with an inoperable brain tumor. As Beth watched her become increasingly debilitated, she prayed night and day. Walking the floors, she pleaded, "Jesus, if you're the same yesterday, today, and forever; and if I called you and you would walk this floor, then you would heal my daughter." Eventually, however, Beth's daughter no longer could talk or swallow. She no longer recognized her father—her favorite person. The only person she did know was Beth.

One day Beth came into her daughter's room in the hospital and busied herself because she was so depressed. As she started to clean the bedside table drawer, she pulled out a Gideon Bible and opened it, longing for something special to read. Growing up in the church, she had learned many wonderful Bible stories, but she didn't really know what else was in the Bible. She thought that was what the preacher was paid for—to study the Bible and preach from it. Beth had been praying to the Lord, but she didn't know much about Him.

Opening up the Bible, she uttered a prayer of desperation asking for something special from Him. As she turned the pages, she came across Mark 16 and read, "He that believes and is baptized shall be saved, and he that believes not will be damned. And these signs shall follow those who believe, in My name they'll cast out demons…"

Oh, Beth thought, *it's not Halloween. I certainly don't need that!* "In My name they'll speak with new tongues." She looked at her daughter and thought, *I can't go to another country and learn a new tongue right now. I've got to take care of her here and now.* "They will pick up serpents." *Now, God…you know that I'm afraid of snakes. I'd never do that!*

"And if they drink any deadly thing, they will recover." Finally, Beth's eyes fell on a part of the passage that would change her life forever. Slowly, absorbing every word, she read, "They will lay hands on the sick, and they will recover" (Mark 16:18, NKJV).

Aha! That was exactly what she needed! Beth laid the open Bible across her daughter's feet, as if she were showing God what He had written. Carefully, tentatively placing her hands on the dying child's feet, Beth looked up to heaven and declared aloud: "God…I'm doing it. It doesn't say pray. Here it says to lay hands on them."

Feeling a little more hopeful, she closed the Bible and finished cleaning out the drawer. The next morning, her daughter went in for another test, a pneumoencephalogram. Beth had no guarantee her daughter would come out alive.

The doctors came out of the test with tears running down their faces. Panic filled Beth's heart; she was afraid she had lost her daughter. They brought Beth's daughter to her room still under the anesthetic. Sitting next to her emaciated daughter, Beth's hot tears rolled freely down her face and soaked her dress.

Suddenly she heard, "Hey Mom, where's Daddy? I'm hungry—let's eat." Beth's daughter was sitting up in bed—completely healed!

"What Would You Have Me to Do?"

This amazing experience sent Beth on a search for more of God. She cried out to Him continually for His help, desperately wanting to know Him better.

Then on Good Friday of 1970, her prayers were dramatically answered. Beth was getting dressed to go somewhere when she looked up and saw the form of Jesus. Beth fell to the floor and cried out, "My Lord Jesus Christ, what would you have me to do?"

A blanket of divine peace filled the room, and she heard the words, "Stand up, for thou art worthy through My Son, Jesus." His eyes were pools of liquid living love. Much more happened on that wonderful day, and that powerful visitation changed her life forever.

Learning to Walk the Walk

After the experience of meeting the resurrected Savior, she couldn't speak at all for three days, but neither did she want to talk. Tears of joy and wonder just flowed down her cheeks. When she did speak, she found that she could speak in tongues, but she didn't know what it was. Then the Lord sent her to a man whom she had never heard of before, a Lutheran minister who lived five hours away. This pastor explained what had happened to her.

When she was finally able to explain to her husband

what had happened, he became very concerned. He, together with their local Lutheran pastor, agreed that it was good for Beth to be seeing this other Lutheran pastor. After all, he was Lutheran, so he must be all right.

Beth and her husband went to see the local Lutheran pastor and also a psychologist. Beth's husband, their pastor, and the psychologist decided that Beth had experienced a pseudo-religious experience before having a mental breakdown.

Afterward, Beth spent five days with her newly found pastor friend and his wife. They pored over Scripture around the clock, and she wrote down as much as possible. She had an insatiable hunger for the things of God. As she was leaving, her new pastor friend told her, "Beth, you must go home, and you must pray often in the Spirit. They think you're crazy. I've had five calls from them, but you must pray to build yourself up in the Holy Spirit. That will be your keeping power. But whatever you do, don't do it in front of them or anybody else, because they won't understand. There is something that you must always remember, Beth; go home and walk the walk before you talk the talk. People will follow after your walk, but you'll lose them with your talk."

When Beth got home she discovered that her husband had taken her name off the charge accounts and the bank account. In those days, if the husband didn't want to be held responsible for his wife's debts, he had to write a letter and have it publicly published—which he did. In addition, Floyd started working nights so he could watch her all day long. Beth, on the other hand, was like a champagne bottle that somebody had shaken and put the cap back on. She was bubbling over with joy, but now she dared not express it. Beth determined she would follow the wise advice of her new friend and "walk the walk."

Secret Joy

The psychologist explained to her husband that after a pseudoreligious experience, people begin to feel dirty and are driven to get clean all the time. So, everyone watched Beth for this cue. Meanwhile, in an effort to not pray in front of anyone, Beth began to retreat to the bathroom and take four to six showers a day, so that she could pray in tongues in the shower. She was so full of joy that she was about to explode. However, this new behavior sent all the wrong messages to her husband.

The local Lutheran church relieved Beth of all her responsibilities, now viewing her as a threat. She lost her church friends, and she and her husband lost their mutual friends. She felt totally and completely alone. Their communication as a couple disintegrated. Floyd was running away from God as hard as she was running toward Him. He and his mother even attempted to have the children taken away from her so that they could have her committed to an institution and give her shock treatments, thinking this was the only way to erase her religious fantasy from her mind.

In the Lion's Den

In the midst of this turmoil, the Lord led Beth to a woman who became her mentor. "What should I do?" Beth asked, fearing for her future in the face of the threat of being committed to an institution. Her mentor said, "Just remember this, Beth: Daniel trusted God in the lion's den, and God shut the lion's mouths. If he tries to take you to a mental institution, I'll pray that God shuts its mouth."

Her husband put her in the car, drove about six blocks, and came back home. "I can't do it," he said.

Beth and her husband lived the next two and a half years in great difficulty. Eventually, her husband too received the baptism of the Holy Spirit—by reading his Bible. After he had heard Beth talk and pray, he had gone to the Bible to check it out...and he read himself right into Jesus.

Pathway to the Secret Place

On the day that God visited Beth, He baptized her with love for her husband. No matter how difficult her husband made life for her, she just loved him that much more. She would get hurt but not angry. She had no one to talk to but her spiritual mentor.

She began to feel that her experience with God had brought a seed of pride into her life because she thought she knew everything, while in reality she knew nothing. Completely alone, except for her children and her spiritual mentor, God was using these difficult times to burn out the dross in her heart. These were her beginnings with God, glorious and yet so difficult. The pathway to abiding in the secret place was a rocky, bumpy, painful road.

Rabbi—Teacher

"Lord, please help me; I don't have time to pray." The Lord was Beth's teacher in such practical ways. She had four daughters of her own and had adopted another. She also cared for three more whose mother had died, and two other girls whose mother was in a mental hospital. In addition, Beth was working full time. She asked God, "When am I going to pray for those you've given me charge over?"

The Lord told her to make a list of everything she did every day. She listed washing dishes every morning, ironing, hanging out the clothes to dry on the clothesline, and making the bed. She took the list of household chores and assigned a name from her prayer list to each chore. Whenever she would work on a particular chore she would pray for the person listed beside that chore.

At that time her husband wasn't walking with the Lord, and Beth admits that she assigned his name beside the chore of cleaning the toilet. But then the Lord dealt with her attitude; He told her, "Beth, you came to the right place, because all those prayers belong in the pity pot." So she shunned self-pity and began to bless her husband, her enemies, and those who hurt her. Eventually the toilet became her "bless-me pot."

A Gift of Intercession

Once when Beth was about to hang the clean laundry on the clothesline, a neighbor dropped by. While they drank some iced tea and talked, she kept thinking about how she needed to go and hang out those clothes. *But how rude that would seem,* she thought.

Suddenly, she jumped up so fast that the basket of clothes went flying across the floor. "You have to excuse me. I've got a project to do. Just wait here. I'll be back."

Beth went to hang out the clothes, and as she did she started to weep, and then wail. She became so troubled that she had to cling to the clothesline pole to hold herself up. The person she had assigned to this chore was her daughter who was in junior high school. So she found herself praying in the Spirit for this daughter, not knowing specifically what was happening. She glanced at the clock as she came back into the house.

Beth's daughter came home from school later that afternoon. As they were washing dishes together after dinner, Beth asked her daughter what happened to her at 2:15 p.m. Looking startled, her daughter began to cry and said that some kids had talked her into running away from school with them. At 2:15 she had gone to her locker to put her things away and get what she needed to leave with them. However, she found that she couldn't move. All she could do was stand there and cry. She had closed her locker and returned to her class.

Beth was left with the joyful knowledge that God had used her prayers that day to make a crucial difference in her daughter's life. Had she not obeyed the inner prompting that was easier to capture because of spending time with Him, she might have missed her God-given assignment.

Grandma of the Prayer Shield

"Lord, teach me to pray," became Beth's desperate cry in those early days. God faithfully answered her prayer. Over the years, the Lord has unfolded to Beth simple yet profound truths about prayer and intercession that she continues to impart to others. Thousands from many nations have been released into ministry as they have learned principles of prayer and prophecy. With gentleness, humor, and simplicity, she captures the hearts of her listeners, encouraging them that they too can hear the voice of the Lord.

In 1971, Beth sensed the Lord impressing upon her the importance of praying for spiritual leaders worldwide. Her vision was based on Isaiah 62:6–7, which reads:

> On your walls, O Jerusalem, I have appointed watchmen; all day and all night they will never keep silent. You who remind the Lord, take no rest for yourselves; and give Him no rest until He establishes and makes Jerusalem a praise in the earth. (NASB)

The following year, Beth and Floyd founded Intercessors International. This gave Beth a forum for sharing her rich insights about loving intercessory prayer as a tool and shield or cover. Besides teaching Beth to pray, the Lord has given her much wisdom, along with extremely practical applications.

She started to be called the "Grandma of the Prayer Shield" when she received great understanding about the need for our leaders to be covered in prayer. These leaders include ministers, missionaries, and business and spiritual leaders around the world. She teaches on many different types of intercessors and, with her great insight, is able to extend grace to others to flow in their own individually tailored intercessory gifts.

Godly Mentoring

Beth highly values the importance of godly mentoring. While her children were still young and at home, she turned down a significant opportunity from the Lord to start a prayer ministry. She felt it necessary to stay home with her children, so she passed that opportunity onto another person, believing that if the call truly was from God, it would still be there when her children were grown. It was.

According to Beth, oftentimes you lay the groundwork and others get the credit, but that's a sign of a good mentor. You don't mentor to *be* somebody; you mentor because God gives you that privilege and that opportunity. A mentor is somebody God trusts. The word mentor means "teacher, guide, coach, trainer, and instructor." Nowhere does it say "possessor." Mentors must never, ever dominate or control. Being a mentor is like taking care of a baby whose bottle keeps falling out of his mouth. The baby may burp all over you and make a mess of things, but if you're his caretaker, you'll make certain that he is fed.

You can't mentor somebody in a class because mentoring requires a heart-to-heart connection. Such connections are necessary to bring out the best in a person, identify his or her giftings, understand weaknesses, and help that individual turn those weaknesses into strengths. "Love bears all things," Paul wrote to the Corinthians. And *bear* means "to carry or sustain." Love also "believes all things," which indicates total faith and trust.

A Servant's Heart

Sometimes we forget the simple things. We forget that Jesus spent His life here on earth teaching us how to serve. He was the greatest servant who ever lived.

We look for an explosion of power, signs, and wonders, and what does God do? In Beth's case, He sent her to be a servant and to keep the house of an evangelist. She had always employed people to clean her house, and then God sent her to clean someone else's. As she did so, she would cry and complain to God, "God, I've got a call on my life, and here I am scrubbing and dusting. How can I do my calling by cleaning these pots all day?"

The Lord answered her saying, "You came to the right place." And He mentioned the "pity pot" again. Conviction hit her heart, and she repented.

One day, the evangelist's wife asked Beth to pray with her, and God spoke through her in a profound way as they prayed together. Later the evangelist was called away to teach on prayer but he couldn't go. So he sent Beth in his place, and that's how she started in the work of the ministry.

Subsequently, Beth poured out her life to help teach and mentor others, traveling extensively, teaching and ministering in seminars and conferences worldwide. Her great proficiency and accuracy in delivering prophetic messages has earned her great credibility among world leaders.

Beth has authored a number of books, including *Becoming a Prayer Warrior, The Mighty Warrior (A Guide* to *Effective Prayer),* and booklets in the Praying with Purpose series. She also coauthored *Intercessors: Discover Your Prayer Power.*

Beth became a core faculty member of the Wagner Leadership Institute and Harvest Evangelism's City Reacher's School. She has served as part of the Spiritual Warfare Network and on the board of directors of Aglow International. She has also been a part-time faculty member at Christ for the Nations Institute in Dallas, Texas.

Beth would not want this chapter to end focusing on her merits. Therefore, it would be appropriate to end with one of her prayers, the cry of her heart.

Father, let Your will be done, Your kingdom come. There is so much information, Father. But we don't want information; we want that which will bring life to Your people, in the name of Jesus, and we give You the praise, honor, and glory in Jesus' name, amen.

Chapter Ten

SHELTER FOR THE SWALLOW

Of all the men and women in the Bible who came to know God intimately, David seems to have been the premier one who understood what it meant to enter the secret place of the Holy Spirit. In Psalm 84, David paints a sensitive and inviting word picture for us:

> How lovely are Your dwelling places, O Lord of hosts! My soul (my life, my inner self) longs for and greatly desires the courts of the Lord; my heart and my flesh sing for joy to the living God. The bird has found a house, and the swallow a nest for herself, where she may lay her young—even Your altars, O Lord of hosts, my King and my God. Blessed and greatly favored are those who dwell in Your house and Your presence; they will be singing Your praises all the day long.

Blessed and greatly favored is the man whose strength is in You, in whose heart are the highways to Zion. Passing through the Valley of Weeping (Baca), they make it a place of springs; the early rain also covers it with blessings. They go from strength to strength [increasing in victorious power]; each of them appears before God in Zion.

O Lord God of hosts, hear my prayer; listen, O God of Jacob! See our shield, O God, and look at the face of Your anointed [the king as Your representative].

For a day in Your courts is better than a thousand [anywhere else]; I would rather stand [as a doorkeeper] at the threshold of the house of my God than to live [at ease] in the tents of wickedness.

For the Lord God is a sun and shield; the Lord bestows grace and favor and honor; no good thing will He withhold from those who walk uprightly. O Lord of hosts, how blessed and greatly favored is the man who trusts in You [believing in You, relying on You, and committing himself to You with confident hope and expectation]. (Ps. 84, AMP)

Often, the Lord has drawn my attention to verse 3: "The bird has found a house, and the swallow a nest for herself, where she may lay her young—even Your altars, O Lord of hosts, my King and my God."

I treasure this psalm, as did my mother and grandmother before me, especially this one line. It has become part of my family heritage. I gained further insights from it through a personal experience:

My girls were taking riding lessons at our neighbor's place. As the horses were being brought in, groomed, and saddled up, I was enjoying myself by watching everyone and all the animals. I happened to look up and see a barn swallow's nest built against the rafters of the barn. *What a delightful find!* I thought to myself.

My excitement was genuine, because my mother had been an avid bird watcher and had taught me to highly value these beautiful creatures for their unique qualities. Personally, I think that barn swallows are some of the most beautiful birds in God's creation, with their iridescent bluish-black bodies contrasted with rich shades of deep orange on their faces, throats, and breasts. These little creatures perform like flying acrobats as they swoop and dive after insects in the early evening light.

As I stood there admiring these fascinating birds, the Lord reminded me of the words of Psalm 84. I found myself thinking, *What an accurate picture David painted of their nature and their nests.*

When a swallow builds its nest, it will first find a barn or other structure with a supply of mud close by. It will carry mud and twigs in its little beak, making trip after trip, carefully constructing a sturdy nest on joist, strut, or rafter beam of the barn. The outside of the mud-dauber-type structure dries and hardens, becoming very solid and secure. Yet the inside of the nest is lined with downy feathers and is soft, warm, and inviting. Instinctively, swallows know how to do this, and it serves them well.

The thought struck me: *Swallows build their nests the*

way they do because, instinctively, they know that the safest place to build is up against the wall. Now we humans use the expression "up against the wall" to describe feeling trapped or being out of options, when we have no place to run and no way out.

We don't have the same instincts as swallows and other animals. God's Holy Spirit leaves us to make our own choices, having shown us in His Word the narrow road to follow. Sadly, we misjudge and miscalculate. Our mistakes and failures leave scars of fear and anxiety, which cause us to think that running away is the only way to stay safe. Oh, that we would learn from the graceful swallow the wisdom of God, allowing our Divine Shepherd's leading and guiding to become such a deep part of us that we can mirror the powerful instincts He has built into His creation. May He weave into the fabric of our lives this truth: the place of abiding is found where difficulty crosses our will and our fear. That is actually the safest place.

To quote an old and wise saying, "Going to the cross is going to the point where my will crosses God's will." How desperately we need to abide in God by "nesting" close to the cross.

When We Are Weak...

Throughout this book, we've been looking at the lessons we can learn from some of history's great Christian women, women who knew how to enter the secret place of the Most High. Certainly, their lives were not easy. These women were not natural-born saints. Every one of them went through trials, persecutions, and testings, just as we do. Now that we can look back on their victorious lives, we have a tendency to see the fact that they walked mightily with God and passed every test, and think, *There must have been something different about her. Somehow it must have been easier for that individual to choose God than it is for me.*

I don't believe that for one minute.

Each one of us must go to the cross. There are no exceptions. The cross is the place where our will and God's will cross each other. The cross is always the place where God's will stands before me—and I am afraid of the pain. I want to run from it as fast as I can.

We do not realize that God will meet us right there—where we are spiritually weakest. If we let Him meet us there, He will give us His grace and strength in place of our weakness.

The truth is, God has designed a cross perfectly for each one of us. He knows the details of our lives, and He knows exactly how to direct us into situations where our natural strength will be tested. He knows how to apply pressure so that every natural desire—those forces in us that make us want to cling to anything but Him—can be exposed as idolatry.

Spiritual storms, winds, and billows will blow into our lives, pulling us this way and that. We will become like swallows tossed around on gale winds, and we'll feel torn about which way we want to go. We will plead with Him—or rail at Him—to make the storm winds stop. Nevertheless, the testing gets tougher.

Sometimes, in the face of winds and danger, we know there is a place of safety in God, but still we don't fly to that safe place in Him. Instead, we fly away, resisting the wisdom that tells us to fly to Him. Why do we all seem to do this? I believe that it's because we all know in our spirits what flying toward Him will mean. We know it will require first going to the cross.

Peace, safety, comfort, rest are found in God, but testing and discomfort are also woven into His design. Therefore, we should turn around and start running toward what is uncomfortable, because that is exactly where we are going to find Him. *We will find our rest only after we choose to nest on a crossbeam.*

David knew this. In Psalm 84, he tells us to fly to that place in God—the secret place, often the place of our greatest testing, known only to God and us. Contrary to our natural feelings and fears, contrary to what the world tells us about seeking comfort and ease, we are to make our nest right there. By abiding in this place, we build a strong history with God. Every trial and storm He brings us through becomes a part of the nest. Day by day, He lines our nest with His faithfulness, His goodness, His mercy, His comfort. We rest secure in His strong tower, built to last.

I believe that if you and I resist the temptation to run away, and instead fly to the cross God has prepared for us, then we will find all the provision and safety we need and long for. Where we are weakest, He will be strong. He will take care of us.

David said, "The bird has found a house, and the swallow

a nest for herself, where she may lay her young—even Your altars, O Lord of hosts, my King and my God." We can rest our "young" in the shelter of His wonderful presence also. Our young may be our children, our dreams, our goals, our ministries, our gifts, or anything we cherish. The shelter of the secret place is not for us alone; it's also a place for those concerns in our lives that matter most to us.

Where Is Your Nest?

A few days after discovering the swallows' nest, I was outside our office, trimming one of the trees. As I brought my blade up underneath some branches, I found another bird's nest.

This nest was nothing like the sturdy swallows' nest in the barn. It was lying sort of haphazardly on a couple of dead, weak branches. The nest itself was really small, and very flimsy. It was made of some dried grasses and not much else.

Immediately I thought, *This is the way most of us build nests. We pick the weakest site—trusting in fickle people who change, or in possessions that break, or in jobs and positions that can be taken from us. We look for our greatest security where there really is no security.*

Not only that, but we build out of the flimsiest materials. We base our sense of well-being on how we feel, on current opinions, and on what this or that trendy expert on a daytime talk show advises—fluff that the world has to offer.

On our own, apart from the Lord, we don't know how to build a nest that's secure. We don't know where our hiding place is. Too often we wait until difficulty comes, and then we frantically try to throw together a nest—a piece of home-spun philosophy here, what Oprah said there—anything to grasp at security. All we can manage to build looks like the flimsy little nest I discovered on the two dead branches outside our office.

Some of us convince ourselves that we're doing okay all on our own. What we've latched onto seems good, but there is a big problem: the nests of security we build out of what the world has to offer are not anchored. They offer no real security, only the illusion of it. When the wind comes, that flimsy little nest will fall apart. Security of our own making grants us no real abiding place.

I am not pointing any fingers here, because we're all guilty. We all start out wanting to find our security in things, people, and positions of power or honor. As Christians we look for security in our churches, our Christian friends, or in our identity as a Bible study leader or whatever. Many of us women find our security in our identity as a wife or mother.

What we need is a place for our spirit that is solid and secure. God's Word is filled with assurances that He wants to be a shelter for us in times of trouble. He wants to be our rock (see Ps. 92), our fortress (see Ps. 18), and our strong tower (see Prov. 18). These are all good images of places to which we can flee when danger has come upon us and we need a temporary hiding place. Yet these are not intended as places to live for a long time.

What's so wonderful about David's imagery in Psalm 84 is that a nest is more than an emergency shelter. A nest is where you can live always. Here you can abide in peace whether everything around you is being shaken or everything around you is calm.

Where is your nest? What do you trust in for your security, peace, and strength? If you know the Lord as your God and Savior, let me ask you: Has He become for you a nest for your spirit, a secure shelter?

Softly and Tenderly

As children in Sunday school, we used to sing a hymn, "Softly and Tenderly Jesus is Calling." He called the apostle John in the book of the Revelation to "come up here." He called the shepherd king David's longing heart into His presence. Throughout the ages and centuries He has called, and one by one they have come, counting in their number Jeanne Guyon, Teresa of Avila, Fanny Crosby, Susanna Wesley, Gwen Shaw, and Beth Alves. With longing hearts and passionate desire, all were drawn to His secret place.

If you quiet yourself and listen, you will hear Him calling you too. David and so many others found their rest at the altars of the Lord. And now it's your turn. Softly, tenderly, quietly He's calling you from the depths of His wonderful presence. How will you respond? Will you join Him in the secret place?

Dear Heavenly Father, I come to you in the name of Jesus, Your Son. I am longing to enter a deeper place of fellowship with you, but I'm not quite sure I know how to get there. Help me find my secret place to meet with You. Help me open up the room in my heart that is meant for only You and me together, forever! Let me hear the song You are singing over the mountains, trying to reach my heart. Give me the song to sing that will so bless Your heart, and bring You great joy. Lord, come, and take all the bits and pieces of my life and my heart, and make them into a beautiful symphony of love of devotion to You! I love You! In Jesus' name, amen.

ABOUT THE AUTHORS

DR. JAMES W. GOLL is the founder of Encounters Network, Prayer Storm, and the God Encounters Training eSchool. James in an international bestselling author, a certified Life Language Trainer, and has taught in more than fifty nations. James was married to Michal Ann for thirty-two years before her graduation to heaven in the fall of 2008. James has four adult children who are married and a growing number of grandchildren. James makes his home in Franklin, Tennessee.

MICHAL ANN GOLL was a lover of Jesus all her life, the devoted wife of James Goll for thirty-two years, and mother of four beloved children. She was the founder of Compassion Acts, a member of the Debra Company Founder's Group, and honored to be listed in the Cambridge Who's Who. She traveled the globe demonstrating that love takes 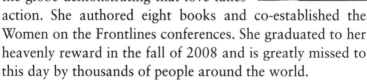 action. She authored eight books and co-established the Women on the Frontlines conferences. She graduated to her heavenly reward in the fall of 2008 and is greatly missed to this day by thousands of people around the world.

EncountersNetwork.com
PO Box 1653, Franklin, TN 37065
info@encountersnetwork.com
615-599-5552 | 877-200-1604

ACKNOWLEDGMENTS

We want to thank all the prayer warriors, pastors and various leaders, staff and interns, researchers, writing assistants, editors, strategic planners, art cover designers, endorsers, publicists, and all the other people who have helped us formulate into words what the Holy Spirit has done in our lives. We acknowledge you. We thank you. We could not have penned and perfected these messages without your help. We do it better together.

The Women on the Frontlines series of books took years to complete. Why? Because these books are not just topical teaching books, but rather they concern the journey of life. Each book highlights the lives of different women from different periods of time and different ethnic backgrounds, with a diversity of giftings and callings. But all of them held one thing in common—Jesus was and is the love of their souls.

We want to acknowledge God the Father, God the Son, and God the Holy Spirit. These books are about Your marvelous hand at work in taking ordinary people and propelling them forward to do extraordinary things.

These books are not written only for those of a certain gender or age or ethnic background. They are about an equal-opportunity God who can take any ordinary life and create a godly lineage and legacy out of it.

Thank You, Lord. May Your shadow continue to be cast!

NOTES

Chapter 3: Jeanne Guyon

1. *Jeanne Guyon: An Autobiography* (Pittsburgh, PA: Whitaker House, 1997), 7.
2. Ibid., 12.
3. Ibid., 32.
4. Ibid., 32–33.
5. Ibid., 33.
6. Ibid., 34.
7. Ibid.
8. Ibid., 45.
9. Ibid., 47.
10. Ibid., 71–72.
11. Ibid., 72.
12. Ibid., 72–73.
13. Ibid., 74.
14. Ibid.
15. Ibid.
16. Ibid.
17. Ibid.
18. *Autobiography of Madame Guyon* (Chicago: Moody Press, n.d.), Chapter 9.
19. *Jeanne Guyon: An Autobiography* 74.
20. Ibid.
21. Ibid.
22. Ibid.

Chapter 4: Teresa of Avilas

1. (This chapter was written with the help of James and Justin Goll.)
2. Bob and Penny Lord, *Saints and Other Powerful Women of the Church* (Baton Rouge, LA: Journeys of Faith, 1989), 161.

3. Tessa Bielecki, *Teresa of Avila: An Introduction to Her Life and Writings* (Kent, England: Burns & Oates, 1994), 17.
4. Lord, 162.
5. Ibid., 178.
6. Bielecki, 20.
7. Lord, 178.
8. Ibid., 179.
9. Shirley du Boulay, *Teresa of Avila: Her Story* (Ann Arbor, MI: Charis/ Servant, 1991), 38.
10. Ibid.
11. Ibid., 39.
12. Bieleki, paraphrases from writings on pages 66–69.
13. du Boulay, 82.
14. Bieleki, 43.
15. Jim W. Goll, *Wasted on Jesus* (Shippensburg, PA: Destiny Image, 2001), 58.
16. Ibid., 68.
17. Lord, 209.
18. Teresa of Avila (Kieran Cavanaugh, O.C.D. and Otilio Rodriguez, O.C.D., trans.), *The Collected Works of St. Teresa of Avila*, Vol. 3 (Washington, DC: ICS Publications, 1985), n.p.

Chapter 5: Fanny Crosby

1. Bonnie C. Harvey, *Fanny Crosby, Woman of Faith* series (Minneapolis MN: Bethany House, 1999), 11.
2. Ibid., 20.
3. Ibid.
4. Ibid., 21–22.

5. Ibid., 22.
6. Ibid., 26.
7. Ibid., 28.
8. Ibid., 32.
9. Ibid., 32.
10. Ibid., 33.
11. Ibid., 39.
12. Ibid., 54.
13. Ibid., 55.

Chapter 6: Susanna Wesley

1. Kathy McReynolds, *Susanna Wesley,* Woman of Faith series (Minneapolis MN: Bethany House, 1998), 68–70.
2. Ibid., 94.
3. Ibid., 94.
4. Ibid., 95.
5. Ibid., 95–96.
6. Bruce L. Shelley, *Church History in Plain Language* (Waco, TX: Word Books, 1982), 354.
7. Ibid., 106.
8. Ibid., 119.
9. Ibid., 120.
10. Ibid., 155–156.
11. Ibid., 157–158.

Chapter 7: Basilea Schlink

1. Basilea Schlink, *I Found the Key to the Heart of God: My Personal Story* (Minneapolis, MN: Bethany House, 1975), 19.

2. Ibid., 33.
3. Ibid., 74.
4. Ibid., 108.
5. Ibid., 212.
6. Ibid., 217.
7. Ibid., 265.

Chapter 8: Gwen Shaw

1. Gwen R. Shaw, *Share My Burden* (Jasper, AR: Engetal Press, 1984), 3.
2. Ibid.
3. Gwen R. Shaw, *Unconditional Surrender: My Life Story* (Jasper, AR: Engetal Press, 1986), 5.
4. Shaw, *Share My Burden,* 2.
5. Shaw, *Unconditional Surrender,* 65–66.
6. Shaw, *Share My Burden,* 4.
7. Ibid., 5.
8. Shaw, *Unconditional Surrender,* 128–129.
9. Ibid., 126.
10. Shaw, *Share My Burden,* 6.
11. Ibid., 7–8.
12. Shaw, *Unconditional Surrender,* 293–294.

PrayerStorm | **The Hour That Changes The World**

Releasing the Global Moravian Lampstand

"Fire shall be kept Burning continually on the altar; it is not to go out."

-LEVITICUS 6:13

The Vision of PrayerStorm is to restore and release the Moravian model of the watch of the Lord into homes and prayer rooms around the world.

Web based teaching, prayer bulletins, and resources are utilized to facilitate round-the-clock worship and prayer to win for the Lord the rewards of His suffering!

Hourly worship and prayer around the world will be maintained with four primary emphases:

REVIVAL IN THE CHURCH

PRAYER FOR ISRAEL

WORLD'S GREATEST YOUTH AWAKENING

CRISIS INTERVENTION THROUGH INTERCESSION

GOVERNMENTAL INTERCESSION

Find out More at:
PrayerStorm.com